THE CHRISTMAS CAROL

DANCE BOOK

by John Gardiner-Garden

71 dances, chorded music, full lyrics and historical notes

3rd edition, Canberra, 2020

This book was written, designed and published by myself, Dr John Gardiner-Garden. I also engraved the music and layed out the book. Tunes and lyrics are either traditional, in public domain or reproduced by permission of specified copyright holders and except for one or two instances the musical arrangements are by Sally Taylor. I composed all the dances (except the one to 'Ding Dong Merrily on High') and hold copyright to all the dances composed and to the work as a whole.

Please feel free to lead the dances and use the musical arrangements but copyright on some recently composed tunes and lyrics remains with the indicated copyright holders and the right to reproduce any part of this work (except for private study, research or criticism) remains with this author.

The work is dedicated to all those who have danced, played and sung these Christmas carol dances over the twenty plus years that this collection has developed, and to all those who share these seasonal pleasure with family, friends and community in years to come.

Privately published by the author
Dr John Gardiner-Garden
Canberra, Australia
October 2020

ISBN 978-0-6450216-2-2

Please contact the author via john@earthlydelights.com.au or www.earthlydelights.com.au if you would like to make comments, ask questions, receive supplements/corrections, extend an invitation to teach, lead or talk, seek permission to reproduce anything in this book, or order further works by this author (listed below).

Also by and available from the author:

Lost Dances of Earthly Delights, Vol. 1: *Pleasures for Four Seasons*, Canberra, 2000 & 2005 (with 4 CDs)

Lost Dances of Earthly Delights, Vol. 2: *Favourites for Four Settings*, Canberra, 2005 (with 4 CDs)

Dancing through the Ages, being a series of 31 books on the dance and dances of the 1400-1900 ballroom, Canberra, 2020.

Illustrations
The front cover features an image from John Leech's *Mr Fezziwig's Ball* (Charles Dickens, *A Christmas Carol*, 1843), the 'Dances by Steps' page a George Cruickshank illustration from 1817, the 'Away in the Manger' page *The Adoration of the Shepherds* by Jacopo dal Ponte (called Bassano), c.1546, the 'Rejoice and Be Merry' page *A Longways Dance* by Thomas Rowlandson, 1790 and the back cover a detail from a mid-14th century manuscript of *Le roman de la rose*. Nearly all other illustrations are from Dover International's copyright-free clip art series.

Contents

Acknowledgements

I would like to thank all the musicians, dances and singers who 20 years ago helped me test and develop the original 64 dances in this collection and all those who in recent years have helped me test the seven dances added since.

I would also like to thank all who have helped sustain our wonderful Christmas Carol Balls tradition over the last 20 years, from my wife Aylwen who has been their chief organiser to all the joyful participants.

I would like to extend a special thank you to pianist friend Sally Taylor, not only for being our Christmas dance scene's musical mainstay over the last 10 years, but for chording all the new tunes and offering suggested revisions to most of the earlier tunes chordings.

Preface to 2020 edition

This work keeps very close to the original 2002 edition that has served our dance scene well for nearly 20 years, but I have made a few minor corrections to earlier instructions, re-engraved all the music (with many chord changes and other revisions) and added entries on seven new dances.

> Ang Pasko ay sumapit / Christmas is here
> Twelve Dances of Christmas / Christmas mescolanza
> Hanacpachap
> Riu, riu, chiu
> Verbum caro factum est
> Walking in the air
> White Christmas

The last one named I wrote 20 years ago but never danced till recently and never published till now. The other six I've composed just in the last 5 years. I have been very pleased with how I was able to incorporate completely new ideas into, and make small unique creations out of, all seven of these new dances and with how well they have all been received. Indeed, my heart is warmed every year by the wonderful tradition that has become our Christmas Carol Ball and the period of practice that leads up to it. With the help of those dancers, musicians and chorister who help prepare a different 20 dances for the ball each year, we have been able to sweep dozens of regulars and newcomers alike, and the family members they bring along, into an uplifting celebration of art, the community and the season.

The following notes made in the Preface to the 2002 edition are still of relevance so reproduced here.

John Gardiner-Garden   October 2020

Preface to 2002 edition

To reconnect carols with dancing and to give people the sensation of once again dancing to singing and singing while they dance, here is a collection of 64 dances to fit popular Christmas carols. Today, the singing of carols offers a rare opportunity for people to feel that they are part of communities - and as a community to sense that they have links to past generations and, through the children, to the future. Hopefully dancing these carol dances will offer one more dimension in which this sense of community and connectedness can be experienced.

Devising these dances has not been a straight 'wham-and-bam' process. Time has been taken ensure the dances are satisfying physically, intellectually and socially. By physically satisfying I mean accessible, flowing, neither too full nor too empty, too tight nor too slack and with a structure and pace that fits the music. By intellectually satisfying I mean easy to learn and remember as you go, with figures and combinations neither too clichéd nor too innovative - new ideas in traditional dance languages - and with a strong storyline). By socially satisfying I mean with attention satisfactorily shared between partners, neighbours and others and with dancers' orientation and perspective constantly changing. In short, I've wanted each dance to be able to be enjoyed in a whole range of dimensions and at a whole lot of levels, and to be fun and rewarding to the beginner and the experienced dancer a-like.

At the same time as attempting to achieve the above, I've aimed in the dance compositions for simplicity, integrity, originality and variety. By simplicity I mean uncluttered, neat and balanced, each dance developing naturally with respect to its motifs rather than having a miscellany of features. By integrity I mean trying to match the style of the dance to the historical and social provenance of the carol and to echo in the dance figures the story implicit in each carol's lyric. By originality I mean not only avoiding copying from others (with the sole exception of 'Ding Dong Merrily on High' to which I've simply put Arbeau's dance for the tune), but also avoiding copying from myself, trying not to use any motifs, knot or combination that I had already used in *The Lost Dances of Earthly Delights*, my collection of 64 dances released in December 2000. By variety I mean making sure the dances in this collection not only reflect something of the historic and geographic breadth of the carol repertoire, but also the breadth of possible social dance steps, formations, forms of progression, moods etc.

To make this book as useful as possible, the material in it has been laid out in as concise a manner as possible. Entries are limited to one page in length and there are four sections to each:

The musical notation given here is intended primarily as a memory prompt, a structural aid. This being the case (and it being impossible to meet all preferences) I've simply put the tunes in the keys in which I play them on my instruments and have given them chords which musicians playing with my band Earthly Delights have developed for them. For those for whom these representations are not suited, please feel free to pitch the whole arrangement lower, make up your own setting, or use a representation from another source. So long as the structure and tempo is similar to that here suggested, it will still work for the dances.

The lyrics are as complete as I could make them and I have presented the first verse and chorus in a way which lines the lyric up with the relevant dance instructions. One exception is that I have kept phrases together even when the opening word or syllable is uttered on an upbeat which might more correctly be though of as the end of the preceding dance phrase.

The dance descriptions are kept brief so as to make teaching in a social setting easy (with at-glance key-word prompts etc) and so that they can relate visually with the parts of the carol text given in the left-hand column, and with the part of the melody represented by the A1, B2 etc in the middle column. I've tried to keep technical terms to a minimum (for explanations of those used see the glossary) and have restricted my abbreviations to the following:

acw	anti-clockwise
cw	clockwise
dsd	do-si-do, going back-to-back
hs / 2hs	hands / two hands
l.f. / l.h..	left foot / left hand
l.o.d.	line-of-dance an imaginary acw circuit around a dance floor
l.sh. / r.sh.	left shoulder / right shoulder
M / W	man or men / woman or women
r.f. / r.h.	right foot / right hand
1M, 2W	The first man, second woman
1s, 2s etc	The 1st couple, 2nd couple etc

The explanatory notes usually include one paragraph on the background to the carol's lyric and tune and a second paragraph on the intention behind the choreography and how dancers might make the most of the dance described. Hopefully the notes help give meaning to the dances, the meaning in turn making the dances more memorable and enjoyable. Indeed, where would art be without context and meaning?

Here then, I hope, is a body of work you can lift from the page with your voice, make stand with your legs, animate with your arms, and enliven with your smiles. Have fun! Happy reading, singing, playing and dancing!

November 2002 (first edition under name John Garden)

John Gardiner-Garden, *The Christmas Carol Dance Book*, 2020

The origin of carols

The Christmas carols in this collection have their origins in many different periods and places (see tables overleaf) The carol tradition itself, however, might be thought to have its roots in very early song-dances. These once had a place in nearly every culture and social milieu. There is probably not an aspect to human life (birth, initiation, marriage, worship, war, death) with which they have not been connected, and they probably had a place in pre-Christian ritual in Europe before evolving into a Medieval art.

The song-dance style of the 13th century English was particularly influenced by the French tradition (English court custom of the day being essentially French). The English they took the word 'carole' from the French, who in turn may have taken it from Italian. Dante, for example, in his *Paradiso* (canto xxiv., v.17) used the word 'Carola' as meaning a singing-dance: 'And as the wheels in works of horologes / Revolve so that the first to the beholder / Motionless seems, and the last one to fly, / So in like manner did these carols, dancing / In different measure, of their affluence (*cosi quelle carole differente-mente danzando , della sua richezza*) / Give me the gauge, as they were swift or slow' (Longfellow's translation). In the 14th and 15th centuries the English went on to use the word 'carol' in a variety of ways - sometimes for a song sung during a procession, sometimes for something approaching a game, sometimes as a virtual synonym for dance. Thus Chaucer in *The Dreame* writes 'I saw her daunce so comely, carol and sing so sweetly'. For more on the carol as a dance see my section on 'The enigmatic Carol' in Volume 1 of my *Dancing through the Ages*).

Where the word carol was referring to a song, the subject could be anything from feasting to politics. Most commonly, however, carol songs had a religious subject, were in a simple unpretentious style, used stock phrases, mixed dramatic devises with elements from the liturgy, decorated honest emotions with exotic folklore, and alternated between the vernacular and Latin. Such songs seemed to have been called for whenever communal movement was at the centre of a civic, aristocratic or church ceremony. The alternation between a refrain (for the people, party guests or a congregation) and a verse (for individuals, soloists or a priest) suited such situations. Carols sat well with the English tradition of repartee (smart reply), of mystery plays and of wassailing (going from door-to-door singing and wishing householders good-health in return for a small gratuity). They sat particularly well with the celebration of Christmas, which like Easter had become an important holiday in Medieval times. Christmas, sitting as it did on winter solstice, a date Druids had celebrated with a feast, Romans the Saturnalia and the Scandinavians the Yule festival, could not but help inherit some of the social nature of these earlier celebrations. Accordingly, unlike Easter, Christmas became an occasion for much feasting, music, liturgical license, well-wishing, drinking and dancing. The separation of song and dance had, however, began. The medieval church frowned upon dancing in church contexts and encouraged a rather sombre music. In the 17th century the English Puritans went even further— discouraging dance in almost any public context and trying to replace popular carols with psalm-based texts. The singing and dancing of carols persisted, but independently. Broadsheets and woodcuts of old and new carols became a feature of Christmas trade, while social dancing manuals by Playford and others became very popular.

In subsequent centuries familiarity with many carols waned, songs separated even further from their dance or movement context, and new more literary carols and new more artful social dances were introduced. Some past traditions did, however, survive. The English tradition of the wassailers lived on in the form of the waits, municipal watchmen who played tunes to mark the passing hours and were licensed to sing songs on special occasions. Folk dancing lived on in villages across Britain and Europe.

In the late 19th century, as part of the general reinvigoration of Christmas promoted by Albert and Victoria (and to no small degree also by Charles Dickens' *Christmas Carol* story), carols, as festive seasonal songs, enjoyed a revival. This revival coincided with important manuscript discoveries and a renewed intellectual interest in the subject. Many fine poets wrote new carols in old styles. A musical tradition which had developed largely outside the church, came inside the church - not all carols for all seasons but a large body of carols for Christmas time. The late 19th century revival of Christmas caroling was followed in the early part of the 20th century by a lot of field collecting - in some cases by people who were also involved with collecting folk dances—and in the later half of the 20th century the genre expanded to include secular songs of seasonal good-will.

November 2002 (with amendment September 2020)

John Gardiner-Garden, *The Christmas Carol Dance Book*, 2020

The origin of dancing at Christmas

As noted above, Christmas sat on a day associated in ancient times with feasting, music, drinking and dancing, so could not but help but inherit some of these same associations. In medieval times the seasonal songs became more liturgical and dance started to separate both from the singing and the occasion, Dancing, however, never totally separated from the singing or the celebration. For a while in some places it became more associated with the end of the 12 days of Christmastide (thus the Twelfth Night masques in 17th century London and the 1706-published dance *L'Epiphanie* presented in Volume V of my *Dancing through the Ages*). By the late 18th century both ends of the sacred festive season could be dedicated dances (thus the 1764 published 'New Christmas Eve' and 'New Twelfth Night' presented in Volume VI of my *Dancing through the Ages*). In the 19th century English-speaking world dancing was firmly associated with the beginning of the lead up to Christmas Day and much sepecial titled sheet dance music was released (see for example H. Farmer's 'The Christmas Quadrilles' presented in Volume IX of my *Dancing through the Ages*). Literature alluded to pre-Christmas balls—for example, in Louis May Alcott's 1868/9 *Little Women* Laurie catches up with Amy at a Christmas ball in Nice hosted by some resident Americans and in Thomas Hardy's 1872 *Under the Greenwood Tree* there is dancing at a party at the Tranter's house on Christmas night. The custom was also alluded to in art and as relevant to where Christmas fell in summer as it was to where it fell in winter. Thus the following detail from the engraving 'Christmas In Australia: Manly Beach on a public holiday' in the *Illustrated Sydney News* of 16 December 1865 shows in the foreground and background respectively the 'Pastoral' quadrille figure and a large circle dance being enjoyed in between picnicers at this popular recreation destination a ferry's ride across the harbour from downtown Sydney (a place where I was born, were I spent my childhood swimming and to which I still occasionally return).

In England one dance became particularly associated with Christmas—the for-as-many-as-will Sir Roger de Coverley. In the early 19th century it was there associated with any ball, but later in the century it was one of the last country dances still featuring at balls and it did so above all at Christmas. It is the dance named as being enjoyed at the Christmas celebration in George Elliot's 1861 *Silas Marner* It is also the dance being enjoyed beneath the Christmas holly in the image below left extracted from an 1882 Christmas Card captioned 'A bright and happy Christmas', and beneath Christmas mistletoe in the image below right extracted from Charles Green's 'Among those who danced most continually were the two engaged couples' illustration for Thomas Hardy's 'The history of the Hardcomes', published in *Harpers Monthly Magazine* in March 1891

We see the three-way late 19th century association of this dance with Christmas and with the nostalgic past in numerous 19th century references and images. For example Charles Dickens in his 1843 *A Christmas Carol* described two dances at Mr Fezziwig's ball during a 'Christmas Past' when Scrooge was a young apprentice (it's not entirely clear how old Scrooge is meant to be at the time of the story's telling/publication in 1843, but we might assume about 40 years was meant to have passed). Fun was had doing a duple minor country dance, with 'top' couples on the way down repeatedly joining with those below in 'affectionate grouping' **But the great effect of the evening came after the Roast and Boiled, when the fiddler [...] struck up 'Sir Roger de Coverley'. Then old Fezziwig stood out to dance with Mrs. Fezziwig, top couple, too, with a good stiff piece of work cut out for them; three or four and twenty pairs of partners: people who were not to be trifled with; people who would dance, and had no notion of walking. But if they had been twice as many—ah, four times—old Fezziwig would have been a match for them, and so would Mrs Fezziwig. As to her, she was worthy to be his partner in every sense of the term... And when old Fezziwig and Mrs Fezziwig had gone all through the dance; advance and retire, both hands to your partner, bow and curtsey, corkscrew, thread-the needle, and back again to your place: Fezziwig 'cut'—cut so deftly, that he appeared to wink with his legs and came upon his feet again without a stagger.** This second dance is the one which John Leech captured in his engraving for the title page and frontispiece of the first 1843 edition of *A Christmas Carol* (turned into a bauble on the cover of this book). The dance is also used to represent Christmases past in the image above right cropped from C. J. Staniland 'A Christmas Dance a long time ago' in the *Illustrated London News*, 16 Dec 1871, p.593. The dance was not, however, ever specifically linked with a traditional Christmas song, just with a traditional all-season tune, so unlike with 'Ding-dong Merrily on High' (where the tune of an historical dance went on to be a well-love Christmas carol—see my entry in this book) I have not included instructions for it in this book. For instructions for various versions of Sir Roger de Coverely see my *Dancing thorugh the Ages* Volumes V, VII, VIII, IX and X.

... and dancing to Christmas carols today

Although in many parts of the world there is still a three-way link between certain dances, certain songs and Christmas (see my brief discussion of the continuing tradition in Sweden in my entry no.72 on **Julpotpurri**), in the English-speaking world the three-way link has faded. Perhaps this book will help reestablish it! Indeed, perhaps, in a small way it already has, because over the last 20 years many people in Canberra have enjoyed dancing the Christmas Carol dances here presented and have come to expect a Christmas Carol Ball featuring these dances as part of their festive season. I've also had the pleasure of leading some of these dances interstate and overseas and have heard of others doing likewise. So I hope these dances can be a source of pleasure for you and your family, friends and community whereever you are.

John Gardiner-Garden   September 2020

Carols by Origin (words / tune)

Medieval or Renaissance sources

Angelus ad Virginem
Coventry Carol
Gaudete
Good King Wenceslas (tune)
In Dulci Jubilo
O Come, All Ye Faithful (tune)
Personent Hodie
Quem Pastores Laudevere
Remember O Thou Man
Unto Us a Child is Born
Von Himmel Hoch, O Englein, Kommt!

Britain

Angels from the Realms of Glory (words J. Montgomery)
The Cherry Tree Carol (words trad.)
The Cutty Wren (trad.)
Deck the Halls (trad.)
Ding Dong Merrily on High (words G.R. Woodward)
Drive the Cold Winter away (trad.)
The First Noel (trad.)
God Rest Ye Merry, Gentlemen (trad.)
Good King Wenceslas (words J.M. Neale)
Gower Wassail (trad.)
Hail Happy Morn (trad.)
Hark the Herald Angels Sing (words C. Wesley)
Here we come a-Caroling (trad.)
The Holly and the Ivy (trad.)
In the Bleak Midwinter (C.G. Rossetti / G.Holst)
I saw Three Ships (trad.)
It came upon a Midnight Clear (double time tune trad.)
Joy to the World (words by I. Watts)
Masters in this Hall (words)
O Come, All Ye Faithful (English words F. Oakeley & W. Brooke, tunes' origin unknown)
The Old Year Away is Fled (trad.)
O Little Town of Bethlehem (tune given here is trad.)
Once in Royal David's City (C.F. Alexander / H.J. Gauntlett)
On Christmas Night (trad.)
Past Three O'Clock (trad.)
Rejoice and Be Merry (trad.)
Sans Day Carol (trad.)
Tomorrow Shall be my Dancing Day (trad.)
Twelve Days of Christmas (trad.)
We Wish You a Merry Christmas (trad.)
What Child is This? (words W.C. Dix / tune trad.)
While Shepherds Watch (N. Tate / G.F. Handel)

Europe

Angels from the Realms of Glory (tune trad. French)
The Angel Gabriel from Heaven Came (trad. Basque)
Hark the Herald Angels Sing (tune Felix Menelssohn)
Il es né, le divin Enfant (trad. French)
Infant Holy, Infant Lowly (trad. Polish)
Masters in this Hall (tune French)
O Tannenbaum (trad. German)
Silent Night (J. Mohr / F.Gruber)
Patapatapan (trad. French)
Riu, riu, chiu
The Rocking Carol (trad. Czech)
Veinticinco di Diciembre (trad. Spanish)
Verbum caro factum est
Where is Santa? (tune trad. French)

America

Away in the Manger (most words of unknown authorship, tune used here W.J. Kirkpatrick)
Carol of the Bells (P.J. Wilhousky / M.D. Leontovich - based on Ukrainian tune)
The Cherry Tree Carol (tune given here)
It Came Upon a Midnight Clear (words E.H. Sears and triple time tune R.S. Willis)
I Wonder as I Wander (J. Niles from trad. Appalacian)
Jesus Born in Beth'ny (trad. Appalacian)
Jingle Bells (J. Pierpont)
Joy to the World (tune by L. Mason)
The Little Drummer Boy (Simeone)
O Little Town of Bethlehem (words P. Brooks)
Rise up Shepherd and Follow (trad.)
Rudolph the Red-Nosed Reindeer (J. Marks)
Santa Claus is Coming to Town (H.Gillespie/J.F.Coots)
We Three Kings (J.H. Hopkins)
White Christmas

Other

Hanacpachap (South America)
Ang Pasko ay sumapit / Christmas is here (Filippino)
Carol of the Birds (Australian—J. Wheeler / W. James)
Merry Christmas (Australian—J. Wheeler / W. James)
Twelve dances of Christmas ('12 days of Christmas' tune but lyrics by J. Gardiner-Garden, dance also called 'Christmas mescolanze')
Where is Santa? (tune French, words of uncertain origin)

Dances by Formations

No partner and trio dances in which a balance of genders is not necessary.

Angels from the Realms of Glory
The Cutty Wren
Gower Wassail
Here We Come a Caroling
The Holly and the Ivy
I saw Three Ships
Past Three O'Clock
Personent Hodie
We Three Kings
Where is Santa? 1

Contras, Beckett formations and Sicilian circles in which you progress with your partner through a set.

Ang Pasko ay sumapit / Christmas is here
Deck the Halls
God Rest Ye Merry, Gentlemen
It Came upon a Midnight Clear 1
It Came upon a Midnight Clear 2
Jesus Born in Bethn'y
Joy to the World
Masters in this Hall
Merry Christmas
Once in Royal David's City
Veinticinco di diciembre
Vom Himmel Hoch, O Englein, Kommt!

Quadrilles *or* Mescolanze, in which 4 couples form a square set, or which start with ranks of 2-couples alternately face up and down towards another rank.

The Angel Gabriel from Heaven Came
The First Noel
Silent Night
Twelve dance of Christmas *or* a Christmas mescolanze
Where is Santa?

Circle dances which mix partner dancing with group dancing and in which you progress on to a new partner.

Carol of the Bells
Carol of the Birds
Ding Dong Merrily on High
Gaudete
Il es né, le divin Enfant
In Dulci Jubilo
Infant Holy, Infant Lowly
Jingle Bells

O Little Town of Bethlehem
O Tannenbaum
Patapatapan
Rejoice and Be Merry
Remember O Thou Man
Riu, riu, chiu
The Old Year Away is Fled
Tomorrow Shall Be My Dancing Day
The Twelve Days of Christmas
Verbum caro factum est
Walking in the air
While Shepherds Watch

Other shaped sets for 3, 4, 5, 7 or more couples, in which you keep or return to your partner.

Angelus ad Virginem
Away in the Manger
Coventry Carol
Good King Wenceslas
Hail Happy Morn
Hark the Herald Angels Sing
In the Bleak Midwinter
The Little Drummer Boy
O Come, All Ye Faithful
On Christmas Night
Patapatapan variant
Rudolph the Red-Nosed Reindeer
We Wish You a Merry Christmas

Couples dances in which you dance with a partner around the line-of-dance and may or may not progress to a new partner.

The Cherry Tree Carol
Drive the Cold Winter Away
Hanacpachap
I Wonder as I Wander
Quem Pastores Laudevere
Rise up Shepherd and Follow
The Rocking Carol
Sans Day Carol
Santa Claus is Coming to Town
What Child is This?
White Christmas

Snowballing mixes which might start with just one couple on the floor but finish with all dancing.

Rudolph the Red-Nosed Reindeer *variant*
Santa Clause is Coming to Town *variant*
Unto Us a Child is Born

John Gardiner-Garden, *The Christmas Carol Dance Book*, 2020

Dances by Steps

Walked dances, possibly also with some slip steps.

The Angel Gabriel from Heaven
Angels from the Realms of Glory
Angelus ad Virginem
Coventry Carol (triple time walking)
Deck the Halls
God Rest Ye Merry, Gentlemen
Good King Wenceslas
Hark the Herald Angels Sing
Here We Come a-Caroling
It Came upon a Midnight Clear 2
Jesus born in Beth'ny
Joy to the World
The Little Drummer Boy
Masters in this Hall
O Come, All ye Faithful
Once in Royal David's City
On Christmas Night
Twelve Days of Christmas
Veinticinco di Diciembre
Vom Himmel Hoch, O Englein, Kommt!
Where is Santa? -1 & 2

Renaissance style dances with singles, doubles, kicks and/or reverences.

Ding Dong Merrily on High
Gaudete
In Dulci Jubilo
In the Bleak Midwinter
Patapatapan
Personent Hodie
Quem Pastores Laudevere
Remember, O Thou Man
Unto Us a Child is born
While Shepherds Watch

Polkas and galops and other dances, even jigs, with brisk step-changes or Scottish travelling steps.

Carol of the Birds
Drive the Cold Winters Away
Hail Happy Morn
Il es né, le divin Enfant
Jingle Bells
The Old Year Away is Fled

Schottisches and two steps with step-together-step combinations or chassees and possibly step-hops.

I saw Three Ships
Merry Christmas
O Little Town of Bethlehem
Rise up Shepherd and Follow
The Rocking Carol
Rudolph the Red-Nosed Reindeer
Santa Claus is Coming to Town

Bourrées and ländlers with brisk triple time footwork and interlacing of arms ('knots').

Carol of the Bells
The Cutty Wren
The Holly and the Ivy
Past Three O'Clock
Silent Night
Tomorrow Shall Be My Dancing Day

Waltzes, mazurkas and polskas with some turning or wheeling as a couple

Away in the Manger
The Cherry Tree Carol
The First Noel
Gower Wassail
Rejoice and Be Merry
Rise up Shepherd and Follow
Sans Day Carol
Infant Holy, Infant Lowly
It Came Upon a Midnight Clear 1
I Wonder as I Wander
O Tannenbaum
We Three Kings
We Wish You a Merry Christmas
What Child is This?

John Gardiner-Garden, *The Christmas Carol Dance Book*, 2020

Glossary of Dance Terms (2002 ed.)

above   Direction in a longways set which is toward the top and the band, i.e. up.

arch   One couple raises joined inside hands and goes over another.

arm   Link specified arms and turn by each travelling forward.

back-to-back   Same as do-si-do. Go past by specified shoulder, sideways behind other and backwards to place by other shoulder.

balance   Sometimes a simple step forward followed by a step back. Sometimes two lots of three steps - step onto first specified foot, bring other up to briefly take weight and step onto the first foot again, then repeat with other foot in other direction.

ballroom hold   Face-to-face, M's r.h. on W's back, W's l.h. resting on M's r.sh., W's l.h. in M's r.h..

Beckett formation   A longway set in which partners stand beside each other facing as opposed to across the set from each other.

below   Direction, when addressing 1s in a longways set , which is away from the top and the band, i.e. down. If 1s need to do something with 2s below then 2s may have to face up.

bourrée   Sometimes a single step (with or without an extra stomp on front foot). More often 3 quick small down steps (l, r, l then r, l, r) with the first being more accentuated.

buzz step   Alternate bending r.knee to fall on r.f. and straightening l.leg to rise on l.toe inorder to scoot cw in a swing or basket.

cast   Turn away from partner and move up, down or around outside of set

chain   Pull past partner or opposite with r.h. by r.shoulder, release hand, extend other to new opposite and pull past by other shoulder. Continue as specified. In a 'W chain' W pull past each other by r.sh. and is courtesy turned by M on other side.

chassé   Sliding step to the side (or on an angle forward), together, step, together.

circle   Join hands just above waist height and move in an indicated direction using whichever step characterises the dance or is specified.

contra   A longways set in which dancers dance with one or two other couples then progress with their partner up or down the set. When couples 'pops' out at end of set they wait out one turn then re-enter in new role.

corner   Near person of opposite gender other than partner - in a quadrille or a circle usually person on M's left or W's right. In a duple minor formation, first corners are 1M & 2W and second corners 1W & 2M.

couple   M and W – and when standing side-by-side the W is on the right of the M.

cross   Change places with partner or opposite by specified shoulder.

crossed hand   M or W crosses wrists with thumbs pointing up and partner takes hold of hands so r.h. is in r.h., thumbs up, elbows bent.

do-si-do   The same as back-to-back.

double   Three steps and then bring first foot up to close without putting weight on it – as in up a double and back.

down   Direction in a longways set that is away from the top and the band.

duple minor   Subset of two couples, 1s starting above 2s, but finishing sequence below 2s, the 2s having progressed up to above the 1s.

fall back   Move backwards with as many steps as specified or as fits sequence, usually away from, while facing, partner or opposite.

galop   Face-to-face with partner, 2, 4 or 8 sliding steps to side. Can ommit final trailing step to ½ turn and recommence on other foot.

galliard   A sequence comprising 4 kicks, a pause, and a spring to switch feet, then repeated starting other foot.

grapevine   A series of steps (usually involving a foot to side, in front, to side and behind) that causes the body to alternate orientation.

gypsy   Move around each other while facing and holding eye-contact. To gypsy by the r.sh. move off to the left and go cw around, by the l.sh. move off to the right and go acw.

hand-in-hand   If to turn slowly or lead, M's palm up W's palm down, but if to turn quickly, clasp hs thumbs pointing up, elbows down.

hands across   4 dancers giving specified hand into a hand-shake hold with diagonal opposite to form a star. Give weight and rotate forward.

high promenade	Side-by-side with partner M holds W's r.h. in his r.h. above W's r.sh. and W's l.h. in his l.h. in front of his r.sh..
improper	When a M is on the W's side and a W is on the M's side of a longways set. In duple minor contras this usually means every second couple, starting with first, is 'crossed over'.
lead	Move forward side-by-side with partner (W usually on r.h.side of M giving her l.h. palm-down into his palm-up r.h.
longways set	Dancers in two straight facing lines.
mazurka hobble step	glide forward on one foot, bring other foot up to meet and take weight and hop on rear foot.
neighbour	The nearest person of opposite dancing gender other than partner, usually immediately to your side.
pavan	A single, single, double step combination, started on l.f. then repeated on r.f..
polka	A brisk travelling or turning step which comprises a hop on the opposite foot to the indicated starting foot, then 3 small steps, starting with the indicated starting foot. Repeated on other foot.
progress	To move on either as an individual to a new partner or as couple to new opposites.
promenade	Move forward as side-by-side couple.
proper	When M are all on the M's side of a longways set and W all on W's side.
quadrille	A square set of 4 inward-facing couples.
rights and lefts	Usually means pull past opposite with r.h. then past partner with l.h. Can be done simply passing r.shs then waist-shoulder wheel. Can repeat back to place.
Scottish travelling step	step-together-step-lift on alternate feet.
schottische	Usually 2 step-together-step-hops forward on alternating diagonals followed by 4 step-hops. The later can be used to turn as a couple by stepping around partner with l.f. and between partner's feet with r.f..
Sicilian formation	A double circle of couples-facing-couples, with couples progressing along or against the l.o.d..
side	With double step approach partner r.sh. to r.sh., then retire with a double. Can repeat by other sh..

single	Step with leading foot, close other foot up to it and take weight on both feet.
skater's hold	Side-by-side hold r.h. in r.h., l.h. in l.h., at waist height. Also called low promenade hold.
sliding	Spring sideways to the right or left, bringing trailing foot up to the lead foot to take the weight. Often repeated. When on done briskly on toes becomes 'slipping'.
slipping	Same as sliding but brisker and all on toes - often used in inward-facing circle.
star	See hands across.
swing	Give weight with partner and pivot cw on r.f., usually finishing with W on right of M.
up	Direction in a longways set towards the top and the band.
two-hand	M offer both hands palm up and W place hers in them palm down, right in left, left in right, thumbs around other's fingers.
turn	Taking specified hs at chest height and giving weight, move around one another – to be quick clasp hands with thumbs up and elbows down.
waist-shoulder	Side-by-side partner M puts r.arm around partner's waist and W puts l.h. on M's r.sh..
waltz	To turn or travel using groups of 3 steps with alternating starting foot. To turn as a couple Ms start l.f., W r.f. and steps are small. To travel in a set start on specified foot and ensuring that the feet pass each other and do not come to a close.
wheel	While side-by-side and facing same way take inside hands and turn as a couple, one forward and one back.

John Gardiner-Garden, *The Christmas Carol Dance Book*, 2020

1.   The Angel Gabriel Gabriel from Heaven Came

♩. = 110 [A] ... [B] ... [C] ... [D] Intro. ... [E]

Cm G⁷ Cm Fm G Cm G⁷ Cm Cm Fm Cm

Cm Eb Ab F⁷ Bb Fm G Ab Fm Cm Gm Cm Fm Cm

Form circles of 4 couples holding hs and numbered acw. **Start** either foot. **Prepare for** walking. **Finish sequence** without having once let go of hs and ready for new couple to right of previous leaders to lead. **Play and dance** the 10-bar 36 beat walking sequence **4 time**s for all couples to have a chance to lead.

The angel Gabriel from heaven came,	A	With 7 steps <u>1s</u> go <u>under an arch made by 3s and invert</u> the <u>set,</u> one person on each side having to twist about quickly.
His wings as drifted snow, his eyes as flame;	B	With 7 steps all raise hs, walk backwards and <u>turn over l.sh. while looping own r.arm over own head</u> and own l.h. joined to neighours r.h. over their head.
'All hail', said he, 'thou lowly maiden Mary	C	Circle the '<u>basket</u>' to the <u>left</u> with 8 steps.
Most highly favoured lady,'	D	With 4 steps <u>raise hs and retire</u> out of circle *while* all except 1M (who remains facing in) pull r.sh. back to <u>unloop arms</u> and finish facing out of set.
Glo...o.....oria!	E	With 10 steps and with no one letting go <u>1M makes an arch with r.h. and pulls with his l.h. so the</u> line threads out until the <u>set is</u> inverted <u>back to facing in.</u>

'For known a blessed Mother thou shalt be:
All generations laud and honour thee:
Thy son shall be Emmanuel, by seer foretold'
Chorus

Then gentle Mary meekly bowed her head:
'To me be as it pleaseth God!' she said.
'My soul shall laud and magnify his holy name.'
- Chorus -

Of her Emmanuel, the Christ, was born,
In Bethlehem, all on a Christmas morn:
And Christian folk throughout the world will ever say:
- Chorus –

This carol is based on a Basque one, 'Birjina gaztettobat zegoen', collected by Charles Bordes and published in the series *Archives de la tradition basque*, 1895. Sabine Baring-Gould, who wrote several novels and hymns (including 'Onward Christian Soldiers') and who had spent a winter as a boy in Basque lands, translated the carol into English, reducing the original 6 stanzas to 4 and giving Gabriel the very beautiful 'wings as drifted snow'.

This is an unusual dance for a figured dance in that at no stage does anyone let go (the only other dance similar in this respect in this collection is the 'Gower Wassail'). Dancers need to be quick off the mark in A1, knowing who's leading, who's arching and who's goiπng to be doing the twist on the side. In the B2 part of the dance it is important to remember that lead M should remain facing in and does not need to unloop his arms in the same way as the others do. All he needs to do is uncross his arms by leading dances with his l.h. under an arch made with his r.h. and all will be back in an inward-facing circle. If all arrive back in such a circle with time to spare, all can simply circle to right (the direction which flows naturally out of the unravelling) till the tune comes around again.

2. Angels from the Realms of Glory

♩ = 100 | A

C   Am   G   C   Am   Em   F   G   C | 1.   F   G   C | 2

B | Intro.

C   Am   Dm   G   C   F   D   G   Am   G   C   F   C   G | 1.   C   G   C | 2

Form a circle of as many as will, no partner necessary, all holding hs. **Start** either foot. **Prepare for** walking and buzz steps. **Finish** all having progressed cw around the circle, but not necessarily having changed neighbours. **Play and dance** the jazzy 22-bar sequence **5 times**, once for each verse, **or as many times as will**.

Angels from the realms of glory
Wing your flight o'er all the earth;
Ye who sang creation's story,
Now proclaim Messiah's birth:
Glor- or,or,or,or- or- or,or,or,or
or - or,or,or,or - oria
In excelsis Deo
Glor- or,or,or,or- or- or,or,or,or
or - or,or,or,or - oria
In excelsis De-e
o…

Shepherds in the fields abiding
Watching o'er your flocks by night,
God with man is now residing
Yonder shines the infant light.
- Chorus -

Sages leave your contemplations
Brighter visions beam afar;
Seek the great Desire of Nations,
Ye have seen his natal star.
- Chorus -

Saints before the altar bending
Watching long in hope and fear,
Suddenly the Lord, descending,
In his temple shall appear.
- Chorus -

Sinners wrung with keen repentance
Doomed for guilt to endless pains;
Justice now repeals the sentence,
Mercy calls you, - break your chains.
- Chorus –

A1   W go in with 3 steps and clap.
     M go in and clap *while* W retire.
A2   W go in with 3 steps *while* M retire.
     M go in arms spread wide *while* W retire.
B1   M wrap wrists or arms round neighbours' wrists or arms and basket
     left (cw) with 8 buzz steps, then separating…
     M take 4 steps out *while* W take 4 steps in and wrap wrists.
B2   W basket left with 8 buzz steps (cw), finish sliding out of basket hold.

     With 4 steps W retire back anywhere between the M.
     All holding hs in circle take 2 steps back and 2 forward.

The text and tune of this carol go back to the French *Les Anges dans nos Campagnes*. James Montgomery, the editor of a radical Sheffield newspaper, *Iris*, and someone who had twice been imprisoned for his political views (for printing a song supporting the storming of the Bastille and for supposedly biased reporting of a reform riot in Sheffield), printed this English version of the carol on Christmas Eve, 1816. Hymn books were soon including the work, but minus the original strongly worded last verse (here included), or substituting for this verse a stanza from another Montgomery work. A tradition also soon developed, which I have followed, of replacing Montgomery's chorus 'Come and worship Christ the new-born King' with the original 'Gloria in excelsis Deo'. Shepherds tending flocks in the wintery hills of southern France had a custom of singing this refrain to one another on Christmas Eve. Although this carol is sometimes sung to the tune 'Regent Square', published by Henry T. Smart, in Psalms and Hymns for Divine Worship (London: 1867), the tune suggested here (now often called 'Iris' after Montgomery's paper) is that of the original French carol.

In this dance you are almost as androgynous as an angel- position with respect to the opposite sex is not important. It is important, however, that the women not hesitate to go in as the men retire out from their circle, that the men, when retiring from their basket, quickly let go of each other's hands so the women can come through, and that the women quickly let go of each other's hands when they retire from their basket to take hands with and fall back with the men. With a big group or with novices you may wish to substitute men's and women's circles for the baskets described above.

John Garden, *The Christmas Carol Dance Book*, December 2002

3. Angelus ad Virginem

♩. = 110 [A] ... [B] ... [C] [Intro.] ... [1.] [2]

C   Dm   C G⁷   C   Dm   C G   C   Dm   C D   G

Am   Am   G   F   Dm   G   G

Form circles of 5 couples. Start l.f. **Prepare for** walking (or skip-change steps) and clapping. **Finish sequence** having all progressed on place around the circle, M cw, W acw. **Play and dance** the sequence **5 times** to return to original partner.

Angelus ad virginem
Subintrans in conclave,
Virginis formidinem
Demulcens, inquit, 'Ave!
Ave, regina virginum;

Coeli terraeque Dominum
Concipies / et paries / intacta
Salutem hominem;
Tu porta coeli facta,
Medula criminum.'

'Quomodo conciperem
Quae virum non cognovi?
Qualiter infringerem / Quod firma mente
vovi?' / 'Spiritus Sancti gratia
Perficiet haec omnia;
Ne timeas, / sed gaudeas, /secura
Quod castimonia
Manebit in te pura / Dei potentia.'

Ad haec virgo nobilis
Respondens inquit ei:
'Ancilla sum humilis / Omnipotentis
Dei. / Tibi coelesti nuntio,
Tanti secreti conscio,
Consentiens, / et cupiens / videre
Factum quod audio;
Parata sum parere, / Dei consilio.'

Angelus disparuit / Et statim puellaris
Uterus intumuit / Vi partus salutaris.
Qui, circumdatus utero
Novem mensium numero,
Hinc exiit / Et iniit / Conflictum,
Affigens humero / Crucem, qua dedit
ictum / Hosti mortifero.

Eia mater Domini, / Quae pacem
reddidisti / Angelis et homini,
Cum Christum genuisti;
Tuum exora filium
Ut se nobis propitium
Exhibeat, / et deleat / peccata:
Praestans auxilium
Vita frui beata / Post hoc exsilium.

A1 With 8 walking steps or 4 skip-change travelling steps 2h turn partner cw once around, open out facing in and take hs in a circle.

A2 With next 8 walking or 4 skip-change steps all into the centre and retire, turning to face partner.

B Clap partner r.h., l.h., both hs, then, *while* turning with 2 steps in and about to face corner clap own shs (arms crossed) and own hs Repeat with corner, turning in and about back to partner.

C Give r.h. to partner and with 18 walking steps (2 for each person) chain (M acw, W cw) 9 hs around set, passing partner l.h. around other side of set and finishing just short of home place ready to take former corner (the 10ᵗʰ in chain) as new partner for 2h turn.

This carol is mentioned by Chaucer in his late 14ᵗʰ century *Miller's Tale*, when he describes how the poor scholar Nicholas of Oxford, kept by his lonely bed a sautry, 'On which he made a nightes melodye / So sweetly, that all the chambre rong, / And Angelus ad virginem he song.' The carol was probably Franciscan in original and brought to Britain by French friars in the 13ᵗʰ century. There is a 14ᵗʰ century Irish source for the Latin version and a Middle-English version that begins:

> Gabriel fram Heven-King / Sent to the Maide sweete,
> Broute hir blisful tiding / And fair he gan hir greete:
> 'Heil be thu, ful of grace aright! / For Godes Son, this Heven
> Light, / For mannes love / Will man bicome
> And take Fles of thee, Maide bright, / Manken free for to make
> Of sen and devles might.'

The Shorter New Oxford Book of Carols' translation of the first Latin stanza is:

> The angel, coming secretly to the Virgin calming the Virgin's fear, said: 'Hail! Hail, Queen of Virgins! You shall conceive the Lord of Heaven and Earth and give birth, remaining a virgin, to the Salvation of mankind; you, made the Gateway of Heaven, the cure for sin.

The peculiar structure of this carol, with a 8 beat phrase in the A part, 5 beat phrases in the B part, 2 beat link to the C part and an 8 beat C part which is repeated, poses a choreographic challenge. The challenge can be turned to advantage, however, when it is realised that a 5 beat clapping sequence can fit the B part and that from the end of the B part to the end of the tune there are 19 beats, just enough to take r.h. with partner and grand chain, 2 brisk walk steps or one skip-change travelling step for each hand, to one place short of home ready to start again from progressed position. A 5-couple format makes not only for a progression in the chain, but also, given that there are 5 stanzas usually sung, a chance for everyone to start dancing with all possible partners.

4. Ang Pasko ay sumapit / Christmas is here

♩ = 120 Intro.

Dm | Am | E⁷ | Am | A- start of verse | Am | E⁷

B | E⁷ | C

D | go to E if continuing | add if ending | A⁷ | E- start of chorus | Dm | Dm | Am | E⁷ | Am | G⁷ | C | F | to A

E⁷ | Am | Dm | Am | B⁷ | F⁷ | E⁷

Form column with couples alternately proper and improper, facing partner across set. Start right foot. **Prepare for** polka steps, walking and doubles. **Play and dance as many times as will** i.e. 8b. intro. +(ABCD EF)xn + ABCD + 3-bar ending.

8-bar introduction			Sway to offer small <u>bow to neighbour on one side</u> (M's left W's right,) sway to offer small bow to <u>neighbour on the other side</u> (M's right) / <u>8 count bow to partner across set.</u>
Tagalog original	English translation		
Ang Pasko ay sumapit tayo ay mangagsiawit	Christmas is here Let us all sing together	A	<u>Man advances toward his partner</u> with 2 polka steps<u>, and takes her right hands over left hand, then</u> with 2 polka steps he turns her cw under joined raised hands <u>into facing cross-hand hold</u> with left on top / With 4 polka steps couple <u>swing cw twice around</u>
Ng magagandang himig Dahil sa Diyos ay pagibig	Some good songs for the season For God is love-that is the reason	B	<u>Man draws woman all the way back to his place</u> with 2 polka steps, then tumbles her acw under joined raised hands into facing cross-hand hold with right on top / With 4 polka steps couple <u>swing acw twice around</u>
Nang si Kristo'y isilang May tatlong haring nagsidalaw	When Jesus Christ was born Three Wise Men came, their journey long	C	<u>Man backs woman</u> with 2 polka steps <u>then</u> with 2 polkas <u>turns her</u> cw under raised joined hands into a wide r.sh. arbour hold, where r.h. is low and left hand is high over heads / With 2 polka <u>turn cw as a couple in r.-sh. wide arbour hold, then</u> with 2 polkas <u>man tumbles woman acw under joined raised hands to reverse arbour hold</u>
At ang bawat isa ay nasipaghandog Ng tanging alay.	And each one of them Offered their gifts to the newborn king	D	With 2 polka steps <u>both turn acw as a couple with l.hs held low and right hands</u> held <u>high</u> over heads, then with 2 polkas man <u>tumbles W cw under joined hs to face l.hs crossed over right</u> / With 2 polkas M draws W back into line with other couples, then all together and with 3 steps (r-l-r) couples push back away from each other to end left foot free
Bagong taon ay magbagong buhay Nang lumigaya ang ating bayan	In this New Year let's live a new life! That our country be safe from all strife	E	All taking hands <u>circle l. with 7 walking steps, then take 3 steps in (r-l-r) and 3 steps out (l-r-l) of circle</u>
Tayo'y magsikap upang makamtan natin ang kasaganaan.	Let us all strive that we may all find Happiness and prosperity	F	Starting right foot all <u>circle 8 steps right, going one place further than starting place,</u> then take 3 steps in (r-l-r) and <u>out (l-r-l) ending in two lines, no hands held, facing new partner across the set.</u>

John Garden, *The Christmas Carol Dance Book*, December 2002

Tayo'y mangagsi-awit Habang ang mundo' y tahimik) Ang araw ay sumapit Sanggol na dulot ng langit Tayo ay magmahalan Ating sundin ang gintong aral At magbuhat ngayon Kahit hindi Pasko ay magbigayan.	Let us all sing together While the world lies in slumber Christmas day has come A child was sent from heaven Let us love one another Let us obey the golden measure And starting today Even not on Christmas day may we learn to give	A-F	Repeat the partner sequence and communal chorus as many times as will
		ABCD (no EF chorus)	Dance with last partner then with 3 steps (r-l-r) push back away from partner and join hands in two straight facing lines
3-bar ending		On first 2 extra bars take 3 steps (l-r-l) forward partner and on last bar while still holding hands in long lines make a dramatic bow to partner in form of nod down and up.	

I wrote this dance in 2018 and am indebted to my dance friends for allowing me to test on them different versions as the choreography developed and for my wife Aylwen for speaking up when she thought the dance needed to be simpler than it was at first. Hopefully this final version, with only two different swing holds (the long crossed arm hold and not-unrelated wide-window hold), with just two steps (polka or walk), and with 'partners' retaining hands with opposites for the nearly the whole of the verse and with their neighbours for nearly the whole of the chorus, will mean even novices can be brought into and successfully led through this dance, and no one has to think too much to create a dance that came be enjoyed spiritedly by all. In this form it was enthusiastically received at our 2018 and 2019 Christmas Carol Balls.

To get into formation to enjoy the dance I suggest you invite all who will to pair up (woman on right of man), form a large circle, then squash the circle on a vertical axis, break hands at the top and bottom and step back a little from opposite couple, so you have couple facing couple down a column, and then invite everyone to start considering the person of the opposite gender opposite them across the set as their partner (not the one they came out with into circle), and to consider those to each side as neighbours. The dance then consists of two parts. The first part is a 'partner sequence' set to the carol's verse music (ABCD) and danced nearly throughout with polka steps. This sequence involves swings with partner in places that are offset from the middle of the column (i.e. alternately in the woman's place, man's place and woman's place) and which ends with the partners all pushing back from the middle of the column into a circle. The second part is then a 'communal circle' set to the carol's chorus (EF) and danced throughout with walking steps. This part ends with the dancers fall back into lines 1 place acw around from where they started, facing a new partner.

The unusual dance starting position and advancing and retiring first part figures offers an opportunity for all the partner swings to have a lot more space then they would if they were to take place on the same axis down the length of the column. To ensure maximum space it is necessary, however, for dancers to remember that the man advances to the lady's side for the first swing, she follows him back to the man's side for the second swing, they both return to her side for the third and fourth swing, and only line up in the middle for that split second that the whole group separates back to home place. To make the most of the swing opportunities it is also necessary to make the most of the transition opportunity offered by the tumble that precedes each of them, as in those tumbles the woman will always be turning about in the direction she is about to continue to turn in the swing, i.e. cw-cw then acw-acw then cw-cw and acw-acw. Although being off-set from neighbors can deprive dancers of a model couple to follow immediately to each siding doing the same as you are meant to be doing, if you look to the neighbours on removed you will see a couple doing what you are meant to be doing.

With respect the music different bands will offer different length introductory and concluding music. My transcription offers the beginning and end suggested by friend, mandolinist and Filipino-music-enthusiast Ian Bull, who introduced the tune to me. All agree that the music for this carol was composed by Vicente Rubi, from Cebu city, in about 1933. There is debate, however, about who composed the lyric. The lyric is usually accredited to the famous poet and lyricist Levi Celerio, but the tagalog version of the carol may have been preceded by the Bisayan language version and have argued that the latter, 'Kasadya Ning Taknaa', the composer Rubi and Mariano Vestil, both of Cebu City where Bisayan is spoken, completed the music and lyric in 1933. The Bisayan version is still popular in the Vistayas and Mindanao region of the Philippines.

With respect the lyric, I offer the tagalog version and singable-translation offered by Dr Quirino Sugon Jr. on his web-page Monk's Hobbit. The carol's original lyrics fit a play of the carol AABC DE AABC, and I originally devised, in order to fit this short pattern, a form of the above dance that was non-progressive but involved using the chorus to change sides. Today, however, many people seem keen to sing verse 1, chorus, verse 2, chorus, and then loop all this several times, ending with a verse. It is this extended structure that I have proposed for the form of the dance offered above. In it the chorus is used to change partners.

John Garden, *The Christmas Carol Dance Book*, December 2002

5. Away in the Manger

Form circles of 3 couples hold hs facing in. **Start** M l.f., W r.f.. **Prepare for** waltz travelling steps. **Finish sequence** W having progressed 2 places cw (one place acw) to partner new man in his place. **Play and dance** the 16-bar waltz sequence **3 times** to return to partner.

Away in a manger
no crib for a bed,
The little Lord Jesus
laid down his sweet head.
The stars in the bright sky
looked down where he lay,
The little Lord Jesus
asleep in the hay.

The cattle are lowing,
the baby awakes,
But little Lord Jesus
no crying he makes.
I love thee, Lord Jesus,
look down from the sky
and stay by my side until
morning is nigh.

Be near me, Lord Jesus,
I ask thee to stay
Close by me forever,
and love me, I pray.
Bless all the dear children
in thy tender care,
And fit us to heaven,
to live with thee there.

B   With 4 waltz steps all <u>circle left</u> (cw) finishing letting go of hs with
      neighbour but retaining inside hand with partner
      With another 4 waltz steps <u>wheel</u> once around <u>as a couple (W back,</u>
      M forward), then reversing momentum....

B   <u>W</u> all go into centre, give <u>r.h.</u> and <u>star</u> around <u>2/3</u> to new M.
      <u>M courtesy turns (wheels) new W</u> in waist-shoulder hold.
      Couples go forward (<u>into centre</u>) with 2 waltz steps.
      Couples <u>retire</u> out with another 2 steps.

Although some believe this carol was penned by Martin Luther, the German religious reformer and author of a number of beautiful hymns, it is almost certainly of late-19th century American origin. Verses 1 and 2 appeared anonymously in *Little Children's Book for Schools and Families*, by J. C. File, Philadelphia, 1885, and verse 3 is by John Thomas McFarland (1851-1913). The tune given here is that most used in England, the 'Cradle song' by American Gospel songwriter W.J. Kirkpatrick (1838-21). Another popular tune for it in the U.S.A. is 'Mueller', probably written by James R. Murray, 1887.

I've matched this carol with a gentle lullaby of a dance, with symbolic cradles, stars and retiring to bed. In A2 M can assist the W into the chain and turn single over own l.sh. to receive new partner (facing the way she is going, letting her put her l.h. on his r.sh.and swinging his r.arm around her waist) and wheel her about. Retain this waist-shoulder hold for the final into the centre and then as you retire slide out into holding hs ready for the circle at the beginning of the sequence.

6. Carol of the Bells

♩ = 140 Just the 1st time   A   x3

Cm   Bb   Fm/Ab   G   Cm   Bb   Fm/Ab   G

B   C

Cm   Am   Gm   Cm   Cm   Gm   Fm   Cm

D   A   just last time

G   Cm   Cm   Bb   Fm/Ab   G   Cm   Gm   C   C   C

Form a circle of as many couples as will holding hs. **Start** l.f.. **Prepare for** rocking and stomping bourrée steps **Finish sequence** having progressed one place, W acw, M cw. **Play and dance** the 28-bar bourrée sequence **as many times as will**, appending 4 bars of dance before the first time and 2 bars at the end of the last time.

Lyrics	Fig	Instructions
Hark! how the bells / Sweet silver bells	__	Just 1st time - W only rocking forward on l.f. as hs swing forward and back on r.f. as hs swing back twice.
All seem to say, / 'Throw cares away'		
Christmas is here/ Bringing good cheer	A1	M join W in simple rocking forward on l.f. as hs swing forward and back on r.f. as hs swing back twice.
To young and old / Meek and the bold		
Ding, dong, ding, dong / That is their song / With joyful ring / All caroling	A2	Take 4 stomping bourrée steps, swinging hs, in place.
One seems to hear / Words of good cheer / From ev'rywhere/ Filling the air	A3	M take 2 bourrée steps out (hs swinging forward) while W take 2 in then W take 2 bourrée steps out while M take 2 in).
Oh how they pound,	B	As M goes back again he lets go with his r.h. and rolls his l.h. neighbour across from his l.side to his r.side, her l.h. now in his r.h.
Raising the sound,		
O'er hill and dale, / Telling their tale,		.
Gaily they ring	C	Swing joined inside hs forward (into centre) and all the way back so W turn over her l.sh. under arcing M's r.arm, then M, turning over his own l.sh., passes W's l.h. into his l.h., then, turns her again over l.sh., this time under his arcing l.arm, and he passes her l.h. back to his r.h., finishing both in a circle facing in.
While people sing		
Songs of good cheer		
Christmas is here.		
Merry, merry, merry, merry Christmas	D1	All take 2 bourrée steps in to centre (swinging joined hs forward)
Merry, merry, merry, merry Christmas	D2	and 2 bourrée steps out (swinging joined hs back).
On, on they send / On without end	A5	All circle left with 4 bourrée steps, stomping becoming quieter as you go.
Their joyful tone / To ev'ry home		
Ding, dong, ding, ….dong.	__	Last time - just M rock forward, back, forward and bow.

The tune for this carol was written by Mykola Dmytrovich Leontovich (1877-1921) and was based on an old Ukrainian melody. The original Leontovich piece (as Judith Otten of New York has discovered) was entitled 'Shtchedrik, shtchedrik, shtchevatchka', described what swallows sitting on the eaves of an inn could see, and did not have a final bass 'dong'. The words commonly used today were written by the American composer, arranger and choral director Peter J.Wilhousky (1902-1978). Of Czech background, Wilhousky grew up singing in Russian-American choirs and made many translations and arrangements of Slavic music. The lyric of this carol was suggested by the legend that at midnight on the evening Jesus was born all the bells on earth started to sound of their own accord. The dance offered here matches the hypnotic trajectory of the carol. Just as it is customary to add voices as the verses compound, so in the dance, the M don't join the dance till after the W have started, and at the end, the M are still dancing a soft rhythmic peal when the W have stopped. In between, each 'plenary' sequence builds up from rocking in place, to bourrée-ing, to turning each other furiously. Indeed the 'gaily they ring' C part of the dance has the M turn once completely about and his new partner twice. This is followed by ringing in unison into the centre and out, and then fades back down to swaying in a circle.

7. Carol of the Birds

♩. = 110

[music notation with chords: C Am Em Am Dm [Intro.] [C] F G C G]

[music notation with chords: Am Dm G C Am F G⁷ C]

Form a wave of as many as will, M on inside facing out holding hs with W on outside. **Start** r.f.. **Prepare for** Scottish travelling steps and setting steps. **Finish sequence** W having progressed 3 places along the l.o.d, M 3 places against l.o.d. **Play and dance** the 12-bar jig sequence **as many times as will**.

Out on the plains the brolgas are dancing, Lifting their feet like war horses prancing.	A	All <u>set right</u> and <u>left</u>. With 2 travelling steps <u>r.h. turn ½ way</u> to finish in new wave (M facing in, W out).
Up to the sun the woodlarks go winging, Faint in the dawn light echoes their singing	B	All <u>set right</u> and <u>left</u>. <u>L.h. turn</u> neighbour ½ way, finishing reaching out to put <u>r.arm around</u> front waist of <u>next in line</u>, r.sh. to r.sh., l.h. in the air.
Orana! Orana! Orana! To Christmas Day.	C	Joining l.hs above, <u>swing</u> in window hold. Finish swing <u>M</u> on inside <u>facing out, spin W out</u> over r.sh. under M's raised l.h. to face in, l.h. in l.h., and turn ¼ acw to <u>give r.h. to</u> next to <u>make new wave</u>.

Down where the tree-ferns
grow by the river,
There where the waters
sparkle and quiver,
Deep in the gullies
bell-birds are chiming,
Softly and sweetly their
lyric notes rhyming
Orana! Orana!
Orana! To Christmas Day.

Friar-birds sip the
nectar of flowers,
Currawongs chant in
wattle-tree bowers
In the blue ranges
lorikeets calling
Carols of bushlands
rising and falling
Orana! Orana!
Orana! To Christmas Day.

This Australian carol was written by John Wheeler, born in Colac, Victoria. Wheeler was a staff writer with the Australian Broadcasting Commission in Sydney, author of some highly-successful verse plays and penner of many songs. He is quoted as saying 'Just as the carols of the old world owe so much to the local colour of the countries which produced them, so it was felt that the new land of Australia - where Christmas is celebrated in high summer - should have its own carols with their distinctive background'. The tune for this carol, as for many other carols by Wheeler, was composed by William James, born in Ballarat, Victoria. After a career as a concert pianist (which began with a London Promenade Concert in 1915) James became the Australian Broadcasting Commission's first Federal Director of Music, a post he held until his retirement in 1957. Of all Wheeler and James carols this is perhaps the best known. The lyric, by reference to daily activity of half a dozen different Australian birds in their native habitat and by use of an Aboriginal word for 'welcome', offers an evocative panorama of a Christmas landscape very different to that implicit in so many wintry shepherd, king, angel or manger-centred northern hemisphere carols. So cock your head, spread your wings and be ready to leap and strut your way through this feathered dance, ending each time through in a dizzy beak-to-beak swing with a new partner, one wing from each touching romantically overhead. Below inSydney Long's 1897 'Spirit of the Plains' European mythology, Nouveau Art and brolgas haunt, decorate and give rhythm to a northern Australian landscape.

8. The Cherry Tree Carol

♩ = 140

(A) C G Am G Am G

(B) Intro. C Am |1. C Am |2 F G C

Form couples holding inside hs facing along the l.o.d.. **Start** l.f.. **Prepare for** slow 'left, pause, right' travelling polska step throughout. **Finish sequence** either with same partner or having taking inside hs with new partner, M having progressed along l.o.d. W against. **Play and dance** the 12-bar polska sequence **as many times as will**.

Joseph was an old man,	A	M travels <u>forward passing W behind him</u>, her l.h. into his l.h.
An old man was he,		M turns W over her l.sh. in front of him <u>back to his r.h. side</u>.
He wedded Virgin Mary,	B1	<u>M puts his r.arm over W's l.arm</u> and they promenade forward.
The Queen of Galilee		M letting go with his l.h. but holding W's l.h. from on top with his r.h. <u>bends down, turns acw</u> under her l.arm, <u>stands</u>, raises his r.h. <u>and turns her out over her r.sh.</u> once or twice while M continues forward to face back against l.o.d..
He wedded Virgin Mary,	B2	<u>2h open turn</u> cw just short of 1¾ around <u>finishing opening out</u>, M on inside, W on outside, holding inside hs facing along l.o.d.
The Queen of Galilee		

As Joseph and Mary
Walked through an orchard green,
There were apples and cherries
Plenty to be seen.

Mary spoke to Joseph
So meek and so mild
Joseph, gather me some cherries
For I am with child.

Then Joseph flew in anger,
In anger he flew;
Let the father of the baby
Gather cherries for you.

Jesus spoke a few words,
And a very few words spoke he,
My mother wants some cherries,
Bend over, cherry tree!

The cherry tree bowed down,
It was low to the ground;
And Mary gathered cherries
While Joseph stood around.

Then Joseph took Mary
All on his left knee;
Saying: Lord have mercy upon me
For what I have done.

Then Joseph took Mary
All on his right knee;
Pray tell me, little baby,
When your birthday shall be.

It has long been appreciated that the Christmas story invites questions. How do we know it was an immaculate conception? Could not Joseph or another man have been the father? If the latter, would not Joseph have been angry? Many stories try to answer these questions. The *Protoevanglium of James* describes how Joseph had doubts about his paternity, he being so old and she so young. The picking of fruit (an image as old as that the story of Adam and Eve, and found also in the finally story of the Finnish Kalevala where a beautiful virgin eats a berry off a tree and gives birth to air, whereupon the old gods flee) also came into stories exploring the relationship between Mary and Joseph. Thus, the apocryphal *Gospel of Pseudo-Matthew* recounts how during their flight into Egypt, Mary, Joseph and the infant Jesus stop to rest under a palm tree, Mary asks Joseph to pick her some fruit, he doesn't want to, Jesus speaks, the tree bows down, Mary gathers fruit, and Joseph asks forgiveness. Similarly, the mystery play performed in Coventry since the 15th century have a scene where, on the road to Bethlehem, Joseph begs Mary's forgiveness after a cherry tree, from which he'd refused to pick her some fruit, bends down in response to her pray. This carol is in this same tradition. It has enjoyed many texts and tunes on both sides of the Atlantic. Cecil Sharp collected no fewer than 8 texts and the *Oxford Book of Carols*, links together three texts, each with its own tune. The Appalacian tune here offered has the feel of a Scandinavian polska, and thus the recommended dance step. The travelling, promenading, bending over, interlacing of arms, facing-off, are all intended to echo the story of the relationship explored in the carol. Note that the W turns over her l.sh. in the A part then in B turns over her r.sh.. Just make sure all turns are wide and smooth and you don't cramp your partner at any stage.

N.B. To make progressive, in B2 turn partner just ¾ cw, then pull on (M along l.o.d. W against) to give 2hs to and tun next along once cw.

On the sixth day of January / My birthday shall be,
When the stars and the elements / Shall tremble with fear.

9. The Coventry Carol

Form longways proper sets of 3 couples. **Start** either foot. **Prepare for** walk steps throughout. **Finish sequence** with top couple having progressed to bottom of set. **Dance** the triple time walking sequence **3½ times**, and as the melody is the same for the chorus and the verses, **play** the AB tune **7 times**, finishing with the same figure you begun.

Lully lullay thou little tiny Child,	A	<u>2h turn partner</u> cw, then all take hs in one large circle.
By-bye lully, lullay.		All <u>circle left</u>.
Lully lullay thou little tiny Child,	B	All <u>circle right</u> back to place, then all take hs with partner.
By-bye lully, lullay.		<u>2h turn partner acw</u> and open out, W on M's right, facing up.
O sisters too, how may we do	A	1s, followed by others, <u>cast out</u> to star on own side.
For to preserve this day,		<u>Switch</u> to other <u>star</u>, <u>M</u> going <u>behind</u> partner to change places.
This poor youngling for whom we sing	B	<u>Switch back</u> to original star, M going behind partner again. Taking
By-bye lully, lullay.		inside hs with partner, <u>tops arch</u> and retire <u>to bottom</u> *while* others lead forward under arch to new position.

- Chorus -

Herod the King, in his raging,
Charged he hath this day;
His men of might, in his own sight,
All children young, to slay.

- Chorus -

Then woe is me, poor child, for thee,
And ever mourn and say;
For thy parting nor say nor sing,
By-bye lully, lullay.

- Chorus -

This tune and text are based closely on ones found in a 16th century source. The carol possibly goes back still further to the 15th century - making it one of the oldest extant ones in the English language. It used to be sung towards the end of the Pageant of the Shearman and the Tailors, part of the cycle of mystery plays performed in the streets of Coventry on the feast of Corpus Christi. In the play the mothers of Bethlehem try to send their children to sleep lest their crying alert Herod's soldiers to their presence. Their lullaby is, however, in vain and Herod's men charge in upon the children. There is some debate as to whether this massacre of the infant boys of Bethlehem ever happened. Some observe that neither Roman nor Jewish records contain any mention of such an event (despite the great interest writers such as Flavius Josephus had in recording Herod's abuses) and that although mentioned in *Matthew 2:16* the rest of the New Testament is silent on the topic. Others suggest that such a massacre fits well with all that is known of Herod and that the underreporting was simply due to the fact that Herod was responsible for so many deaths in so many places. Whatever the case, this carol offers a rare insight into the type of biblical story that had resonance for the common folk of renaissance England. The refrain, as in many of these older carols, appears to have been an opportunity for fuller community participation in the song and the expression of feeling it carried.

This dance attempts to capture the carol's story of love and grief. The chorus of the dance is charged with tender cradling and being-pulled-in-different-directions motifs. The verses of the dance use a small-scale version of a German folkdance mill figure to generate images of searching, bewilderment and loss - couples parting, casting this way and that, then retiring helplessly to the bottom of the set. To assist in smoothly switching between stars the two stars should be as close as possible, even interleafed - like a pair of cogs. To fully capture the poignancy it is suggested dancers use an unfaulting smooth walking step throughout and make all turns as wide as possible. It is almost too sad to dance.

10. The Cutty Wren

Form two concentric circles of approximate equal number of M and W, M holding hs on outside facing in, W on inside facing out, no partner necessary. **Start** l.f. **Prepare for** running bourrée steps. **Finish sequence** resuming hs with same neighbours but having changed circles. **Play and dance** the 16-bar bourrée sequence as many times as will.

'Where are we going?' says Milder to Melder.	A1	With 12 running steps <u>all go left</u> in own circle, outside circle cw, inside circle acw.
'Where are we going?' says vassal to foe.	A2	Outside circle <u>closes</u> <u>in</u> *while* inside circle reverses even further into the centre, and as dancers in both circle do so they <u>raise</u> their <u>joined hs</u>, <u>look</u> to their <u>right and loop</u> their now slack <u>arms over</u> their own <u>heads</u>, own l.arm over own head onto own r.sh..
'We may not tell you,' says the younger to the elder.	B	With 12 running steps and leaning out a little <u>all basket</u> in this 'cage' or 'net' formation to the <u>right</u>, along l.o.d.
'Away to the green wood!' says John the Red Nose.	A3	All raise hs, <u>let go and turn 1½ over l.sh.</u>, those on the inside escaping between gaps to take hs in a new inward-facing outside circle and those outside taking hs in a new outward-facing inside circle - in other words, <u>swapping circles</u>.

'What shall we do there?' says...
'What shall we do there?' says ….
'We may not tell you,' says ….
'Hunt for the Cutty Wren!' says ...

'How shall we shoot her?' says.
'With bows and with arrows,' says ….
'That will not do, then,' says
'With big guns and with cannon!' says..

'How shall we fetch her home?' says…
'On four strong men's shoulders,' says..
'That will not do, then,' says ….
'In oxcarts and in wagons!' says ….

'How shall we cut her up?' says …..
'With forks and with knives,' says …
'That will not do, then,' says…
'With hatchets and with cleavers!' says...

'How shall we cook her?' says …
'In pots and in kettles,' says …
'That will not do, then,' says ….
'In a bloody great brass cauldron!' says...

'Who'll get the spare ribs?' says ….
'Who'll get the spare ribs?' says ….
'We may not tell you,' says ...
'We'll give 'em all to the poor!' says...

This 'Day after Christmas' carol is a relic of an ancient custom. For centuries in many parts of Britain and Ireland December 26, St Stephen's Day, was as important as Christmas day and was the day for 'Hunting the Wren' or 'Going on the Wren'. Groups of boys would look for a wren then chase it until caught. The dead bird was tied to the top of a pole or holly bush, decorated with ribbons or coloured paper and carried around the village. At each house the boys, wearing straw masks or blackened faces, and dressed in old clothes, would sing a song and receive money. There were various songs, including one which began:

> The wren, the wren is king of the birds
> St Stephen's Day he's caught in the furze
> Although he is little his family is great
> We pray you, good landlady, give us a treat!

How the wren hunting custom came about is not clear. Some say that St Stephen, hiding from his enemies in a bush, was betrayed by a chattering wren, so the bird, like St Stephen, should be hunted down and stoned to death. Some that it is punishment for the wren betraying, albeit accidentally, Irish warriors sneaking up on the camp of some invading Vikings. Others that the killing of the wren, the 'king of the birds', is related to the pagan custom of sacrificing something sacred at year's end (or indeed a king every seven years) for the good of the tribe and land. Whatever the origin, the custom has been revived in some places in recent years, with girls joining boys to parade an artificial wren or a real wren in a cage and collect money (e.g. for their community or school).

To match this children's song, I have devised a dance which mimes children trying to trap some birds then setting them flitting (into exchanged roles). It is suitable for children, not needing exactly the same number of boys as girls, and not requiring boys and girls to hold each other's hs. The more dancers, however, the more comfort the cages.

John Garden, *The Christmas Carol Dance Book*, December 2002

11. Deck the Halls

Form a Beckett formation contra set of as many couples as will, partners side-by-side, holding hs in long line. **Start** either foot. **Prepare for** brisk walking and setting steps. **Finish sequence** progressed as a couple one place acw around the set. **Play and dance** the 16-bar walking sequence **as many times as will** (4 times will exhaust the verses, but these can then be repeated).

Deck the halls with boughs of holly.
Fa la la la la, la la la la
'Tis the season to be jolly.
Fa la la la la, la la la la
Don we now our gay apparel.
Fa la la la la, la la la la
Troll the ancient Yule-tide carol.
Fa la la la la, la la la.

See the blazing Yule before us.
Fa la la la la, la la la la
Strike the harp and join the Chorus.
Fa la la la la, la la la la
Follow me in merry measure.
Fa la la la la, la la la la
While I tell of Yule-tide treasure.
Fa la la la la, la la la.

Fast away the old year passes.
Fa la la la la, la la la la
Hail the new year, lads and lasses
Fa la la la la, la la la la
Sing we joyous, all together.
Fa la la la la, la la la la
heedless of the wind and weather.
Fa la la la la, la la la.

(fun Latin verse)

Aquafolia ornatis
Fa la la la la, la la la la
Tempus hoc hilaritatis
Fa la la la la, la la la la
Vestes claras induamus;
Fa la la la la, la la la la
Cantilenas nunc promamus
Fa la la la la, la la la.

A1 Forward with 4 steps raising joined hs to touch opposites hs.
    With hs held high and wide, set right and left.
A2 Retire with 4 steps, lowering arms but holding hs in line.
    Set right and left.
B   Those who can change r.h. with own gender on r.diagonal.
    All change l.h. across set with opposite gender person.
    Those who can change r.h. to change on r. diagonal.
    L.h. to change across and finish side-by-side with partner facing new opposite.

The text is a very free translation of Nos Galan, a Welsh dance-carol or *canu penillion* traditionally sung at New Year's Eve. The tune spread more widely in the 18th century and was used in a violin and piano duet by Mozart. It turned into a traditional English Christmas song as part of the Victorian re-invention of Christmas in the late 19th century- a phenomenon also experienced in the America of that time. The first English version appeared in The Franklin Square Song Collection edited by J.P. McCaskey in 1881. There have been many subsequent versions- and I've here added on a Latin verse by Stanford Miller.

It is not known what steps were danced to the original Welsh carol - only that it was in a circle around a harp, probably involved dancers contributing verses and the harp responding with the chorus. Dancers might have had to drop out when invention failed and nonsense syllables such as Fa-la-la-la-la might have substituted for a harp in the absence of a harpist. I have taken the liberty of devising a dance in an English formation not often used these days but once common - a longways set where instead of having partner opposite you in the other line of set, your partner is beside you (called the 'Beckett' formation in modern-day Amercian contra dancing). To avoid confusion in the chaining part of the dance I suggest dancers not let go of their r.h. after the change on the diagonal till they have taken l.hs across the set, and not release their l.h. after the pull across the set till they have again taken r.h. on the diagonal. Couples progress somewhat magically acw around the set, so those who were on the right hand end of one line will, after once through the dance, be on the left hand end of the opposite line facing back towards original side. If 4 couples in small set (2 couples on each side) then by the time 4 verses are sung (would need to include the Latin one) all would be back in starting place. The dance can, however, be enjoyed by many more couples for much longer by just repeating verses.

John Garden, *The Christmas Carol Dance Book*, December 2002

12. Ding Dong Merrily on High

Form a circle of as many couples as will holding hs. **Start** l.f. **Prepare for** single, double and women jumping. **Finish sequence** with weight on r.f. ready to go left again, W having progressed 2 places cw around circle. **Play and dance** the 24-bar branle sequence **as many times as will**.

Ding dong, merrily on high,
In heav'n the bells are ringing.
Ding dong, verily the sky
Is riv'n with angel singing:
Glor - or,or,or,or - or - or,or,or,or
or - or,or,or,or - oria
Hosanna in excelsis
Glor - or,or,or,or - or - or,or,or,or
or - or,or,or,or - oria
Hosanna in excelsis

E'en so here below, below
Let steeple bells be swungen
And I-o, I-o, I-o
By priest and people be sungen:
- Chorus -

Pray you dutifully prime
Your matin chime, ye ringers.
May ye beautifully rhyme
Your evetime song, ye singers:
- Chorus –

A1   <u>Double left</u> (3 steps and close) swinging hs in & back twice.
       <u>Double right</u> swinging hs forward and back twice.
A2   <u>Repeat</u> A1.

B1   <u>6 singles (step, close) left</u>, swinging hs in and back each single, then M puts hs on waist of W on right, she her hs on his shs.
       W jumps *while* <u>M guides W</u> across <u>to his l.h.side</u>.
B2   <u>Repeat</u> 6 singles and jump, finishing with the W having made a double progression acw around the circle.

This carol is a good example of a carol in the original sense of the word (i.e. a secular dance tune) evolving into a carol as it is understood today (i.e. a song for Christmas). The tune first appeared in the *Orchesographie*, a dance book written by Johan Tabourot (1519-93), a canon of Langres, under the anagram Thoinot Arbeau. 'Branle l'Officiel' was to be danced by 'lackeys and serving wenches and sometimes by young men and maids of gentle birth masquerading as peasants and shepherd'. The dance title, though sometimes translated as 'The Official Branle' or 'The Officers' Brawl' ('brawl' being the appropriate translation of 'branle'), might better be translated as 'The servants' hall (*l'office*) Branle/Brawl'. The very Victorian archaic English lyric was composed early in the 20th century by George Ratcliffe Woodward (1848-1934), the author of several carol books - and someone particularly interested in rehabilitating tunes found in the 16th century Finnish collection, *Piae Cantiones*.

For the dance, Arbeau describes the men as taking the women under her bust and lifting her into the air, but suggests you can substitute for this a kiss. In the above version of the dance, popular in medieval recreation circles today, the lifting of the woman turns into 'lift and passing around', in short a 'throw', so that the women progress to a new position and new partner with every lift. I've also added the bell-like forward and back swinging of joined hs to complement the ringing imagery we now associate with the tune thanks to Woodward's immortal verse.

13. Drive the Cold Winter Away

Form a double circle of couples facing along l.o.d. holding inside hs. **Start** outside foot. **Prepare for** one slow polka step per bar. **Finish sequence** having travelled with your partner a little along the line-of-dance (option of taking new partner at end, M progressing along l.o.d., W against). **Play and dance** the 16-bar jig sequence **as many times as will**.

All hail to the days
that merit more praise
Than all the rest of the year.

And welcome the nights
that double delights
As well for the poor as the peer.

Good fortune attend
each merry man's friend

Each does but the best that he may
Forgetting all wrongs with poems and
songs / To drive the cold winter away.

A1 With one polka step turn out to be back to back and with a second polka step slide along l.o.d.
Taking hold of both hs back-to-back balance (with 2 polka steps) against and along l.o.d (M onto l.f. then r.f., W r.f. then l.f.) .

A2 With 1 polka step turn back to be face-to-face and, taking 2hs open hold, with another polka step balance against l.o.d.
With 2 more polka steps balance along and against l.o.d.

B1 With two polka steps turn solo once about over outside shoulder (M l.sh., W r.sh.) W in place, M travelling along l.o.d. to take new partner in ballroom hold.
With new partner balance along then against l.o.d.

B2 Turn as a couple twice about with 4 polka steps.

Tis ill for the mind to anger incline
To think of small injuries now. / If
wrath be to seek, don't lend her thy
cheek / Don't let her inhabit thy
brow. / Cross out of thy books
malevolent looks / Both beauty and
youth decay. And spend the long
night in honest delight
To drive the cold winter away.

When Christmas tide comes in like
a bride / with holly and ivy clad.
Twelve days in the year must mirth
and good cheer / In every
household is had. / The popular
guise is then to devise / All manner
of Christmas games. / Both women
and men do best that they can /
To drive the cold winter away.

This time of the year is spent in
good cheer, / With neighbours who
gather to meet. / Just sit by the fire
with friendly desire / With others in
love to greet. / All grudges forgot
are put in the pot / All sorrows aside
they lay. / The old and the young do
carol this song /
o drive the cold winter away.

The verses given here for this carol are drawn from 17th and 18th century versions of an English ballad which went by various names - including 'All Hayle to the Days' and 'When Phoebus did Rest'. An original version can be found in a broadside collection under the heading 'A Pleasant Country new Ditty: Merrily shewing how to drive the cold winter away'. Versions of tune can be found in several sources, including John Playford's 1651 *The English Dancing Master*. There the tune is a lively jig to accompany a three-part longways dance. In he Playford dance only the couples at each end of the set get to do much dancing and there is no progression of lead or position to help share the action. To give all an opportunity to dance with everyone I have written a very different dance to go to the tune, and one which picks up some of the imagery from the carol's lyric. In the A part you can image warming yourself in front of fire (your partner), first your back then your front. In the B part of the dance you have the image of going outside, being blown around then, warming up dancing as a couple.

If the tune is played as a lively jig, as its 17th century associations suggest it should be, then it can be danced comfortably using polka or Scottish-travelling steps. If the tune is played more slowly, as many musicians are want to play it these days, these polka steps become more chassé steps or leisurely step-together-step-lift steps.

Thus none will allow of solitude now, / But merrily greets the time,
To make it appeare / Of all the whole yeare
That this is accounted the Prime.
December is seene / Apparel'd in greene And January, fresh as May,
Comes dancing along / With a cup or a Song
To drive the cold winter away.

John Garden, *The Christmas Carol Dance Book*, December 2002

14. The First Noel

Form circles of 3 couples, numbered acw. **Start** M start l.f., W either foot. **Prepare for** travelling waltz steps throughout. **Finish sequence** W having progressed one place acw. **Play and dance** the 24-bar waltz sequence **9 times**, 1M leading with each of the 3 women, then 2 M leading with each woman, then 3M.

The first Noel
the angel did say
Was to certain poor shepherds
in fields as they lay;
In fields where they lay
akeeping their sheep
On a cold winter's night
that was so deep.
Noel, Noel,
Noel, Noel,
Born is the King
of Israel.

A1   With 4 waltz steps <u>1s 2h turn</u>.

<u>1M lead</u> 1W <u>between 2s</u> and around behind then in front of 2M, 1M finishing facing and joining hs with 2W.

A2   <u>1s and 2s circle</u> left ¾ and 1M then lead 1W, 2M & 2W towards 3s.

<u>1M lead between 3s</u> behind 3M and then back around set towards place.

B   <u>All</u> joining hs <u>circle left 2/3</u>, finishing one place short of original position.
<u>M solo turn</u> over l.sh. <u>in front of W</u> on left to home place.
<u>All bow</u> to new partner, W having progressed one place acw.

They looked up / and saw a star
Shining in the East, / beyond them far;
And to the earth / it gave great light,
And so it continued
both day and night.
- Chorus -

And by the light / of that same star,
Three wise men came
from country far;
To seek for a King / was their intent,
And to follow the star
wherever it went.
- Chorus -

This star drew nigh / to the northwest,
O'er Bethlehem it / took its rest,
And there it did / both stop and stay
Right over the place / where Jesus lay.
- Chorus -

Then did they know / assuredly
Within that house / the King did lie;
One entered in / for them to see
And found the babe / in poverty.
- Chorus -

Then entered in / those wise men three,
Full reverently / upon their knee;
And offered there / in his presence,
Their gold, and myrrh,/ and frankincense.
- Chorus -

This combination of tune and lyrics first appeared in William Sandys' Christmas Carols, *Ancient and Modern* (London, 1833), but Sandys took it almost verbatim from an 1823 work by Davies Gilbert called *Some Ancient Christmas Carols*. Davies in turn took it from an 1817 manuscript collection of Cornish carols. The carol may indeed go all the way back to 13th century miracle plays ('Noel', the French word for Christmas, coming from the Latin *natalis* meaning 'pertaining to birth') - but the curious structure of the tune has led some to believe that it is in fact a conflation of a melody of one tune with a harmony of another.

To match the lyric, here is a flowing dance in which you get to play shepherds and sheep. 1M leads three times (each time with different W) then, when all back to original partner, 2M leads three times, then 3M lead. For good male dancers, there is an opportunity towards the end of the sequence to dance like kings, hs in the air (perhaps holding an invisible crown) when the men twirl on to new position and a new partner. If 9 times through the tune and dance is hard to sustain, then you can just do a 3 times through version - either without the M changing partners and each M taking a turn to lead or with the M changing partners but with just the 1M leading each time.

Between an ox stall / and an ass, /This Child truly / there born he was; For want of clothing / they did him lay / All in the manger, / among the hay. / -Chorus –

Then let us all / with one accord / Sing praises to our / Heavenly Lord, That hath made heaven / and earth of naught, / And with his blood / mankind hath bought. / - Chorus -

If we in our time / shall do well, / We shall be free from / death and Hell, For God hath prepared / for us all / A resting place / in general. / - Chorus -

John Garden, *The Christmas Carol Dance Book*, December 2002

15. Gaudete

♩ = 130

(musical notation)

Chords under staff A: Dm Am Dm C F C Dm Am Am Dm C Dm Am B♭ C Gm Am Dm

Chords under staff B: Dm F B♭ Gm D Gm E♭ B♭ Dm A Dm (Intro.)

Form a double circle of as many couples as will, M on inside facing out holding r.h. in r.h. with W on outside facing in. **Start** l.f. **Prepare for** singles, doubles and reverences. **Finish sequence** all having progressed one place, M against, W along l.o.d., ready to turn new partner with r.h. **Play** the tune **and dance** the sequence **as many times as will**.

Gaudete, gaudete *Christus est natus* *Ex Maria virgine, gaudete.*	A1	½ r.h. turn partner with a l.f. double <u>then</u>, releasing hs., step back from partner with a <u>r and l</u>, bend l.knee <u>and reverance</u> pointing r.f. ½ <u>l.h. turn</u> partner back to home place with r.f. double, <u>then</u> release hs, step back from partner with a <u>l and r</u>, bend r.knee <u>and reverance</u> pointing l.f.
Repeat chorus	A2	Repeat A part of dance
Tempus ad est gratiae	B	<u>Double forward on own left diagonal to form a wave</u>, M facing out W in, all holding r.h. in r.h. with original partner, l.h. in l.h. with corner.
Hoc quod optabamus		In wave, <u>balance right</u> (step onto right and kick left across) <u>and left</u> (step with left back to left and kick r.f. across).
Carmina laetitiae		<u>Double to own right</u> across in front of partner to form a new wave, l.h. in l.h. with original partner, r.h. in r.h. with new corner.
Devote redamus.		<u>Balance left and right,</u> finishing holding r.hs with new partner.

- Chorus -
Deus homo factus est
Natura mirante,
Mundus renovatus est
A Christo regnante.

- Chorus -
Ezechielis porta
Clausa pertransitur
Unde lux est orta
Salus invenitur.

- Chorus -
Ergo nostra contio
Psallat jam in lustro,
Benedicat domino
Salus regi nostro.

The verses of this carol derive from the medieval Bohemian song 'Ezechielis porta', a song which may have been heard by Finnish clerical students studying in Prague. Finno, the editor of *Piae Cantione*, included the verses in his book, adding a refrain which he may himself have adapted from a Lutheran German song. The *Shorter New Oxford Book of Carols* translates the text as follows:

Rejoice! Rejoice! Christ is born of the Virgin Mary; rejoice!
1. The time of grace has come for which we have prayed; let us devoutly sing songs of joy.
2. God is made man, while nature wonders; the world is renewed by Christ the King.
3. The closed gate of Ezekiel has been passed through; from where the Light has risen [the East] salvation is found.
4. Therefore let our assembly sing praises now at this time of purification; let it bless the Lord: greetings to our King.

This dance uses basic Renaissance steps such as doubles, singles and reverences, but combines them in such a way as to create a very lively social mixer. The giving of right and left hs in the A part encourages dancers to look at their partners and the jazzy sideways doubles and singles (chassés and balances) in wave formation in the B part offer an opportunity for the group as a whole to share weight and dance together. On those occasions when musician or singers want to repeat the A part of the tune (because the structure AAB is as common as AB), dancers simply repeat the A part of the dance - but they should be encouraged to take more extravagent steps and make more expansive reverences the second time through.

16. God Rest Ye Merry, Gentlemen

Form longways improper duple minor sets of as many as will facing partner. **Start** r.f.. **Prepare** for walking step throughout. **Finish sequence** with 1s having progressed as a couple one place down set and 2s one place up set. **Play and dance** the 20-bar jig-walking sequence **as many times as will**.

God rest you merry, gentlemen,
Let nothing you dismay,
Remember Christ our Savior
Was born on Christmas day,
To save us all from Satan's pow'r
When we were gone astray:
O tidings of comfort and joy
Comfort and joy,
O tidings of comfort and joy.

From God our heavenly Father
A blessed angel came.
And unto certain shepherds
Brought tidings of the same,
How that in Bethlehem was born
The Son of God by name: - *Chorus* -

'Fear not', then said the angel,
'Let nothing you afright,
This day is born a savior,
Of virtue, power, and might;
So frequently to vanquish all
The friends of Satan quite'; - *Chorus* -

The shepherds at those tidings
Rejoiced much in mind,
And left their flocks a-feeding,
In tempest, storm, and wind,
And went to Bethlehem straightway
This blessed babe to find: - *Chorus* - .

But when to Bethlehem they came,
Whereat this infant lay,
They found him in a manger,
Where oxen feed on hay;
His mother Mary kneeling,
Unto the Lord did pray: - *Chorus* -

Now to the Lord sing praises,
All you within this place,
And with true love and brotherhood
Each other now embrace;
This holy tide of Christmas
All others doth deface: - *Chorus* -

A1   Long lines go forward and back.

A2   With 8 steps circle left below (1s with 2s), finishing pulling corner/neighbour into ballroom hold.

B   Swing neighbour, finish W on right of M facing down, sliding out into holding hs.

C   With 4 steps down the hall 4-in-line, then with 4 steps turn as a couple, W under M's r.h.,
With 4 steps return back up in a line-of-4 then with 4 steps 1s dropping inside hs and wheel back into contrary lines.

In Charles Dickens' *A Christmas Carol* Ebenezer Scrooge hears this carol being sung outside his door and, shunning all that's cheerful, threatens to hit the singer with a ruler if he does not desist immediately. It is indeed a merry number for a tune in a minor key. There are, however, no 'merry gentlemen' in the song. A comma can be very important. The verse does not exhort 'merry Gentlemen' to rest, but rather reassures ('rest merry') the shepherds (verse 5) who are frightened by the sudden appearance of an angel. There are many versions, including parodies. The one here printed is from William Sandys' 1833 *Christmas Carols, Ancient and Modern,* though omitting, as is common, Sandys' second verse (not essential to the story). The lyrics probably go back to those sung by the municipal watchmen in Old England, the waits. The tune to which the carol was originally sung is unknown but today it is nearly always sung to one known as the 'London tune', first printed in 1846 and given its present form in Bramley and Stainer's *Christmas Carols, New and Old*, 1871. This tune (printed above) had already seen service carrying many other carols and songs in England and North America, and has been traced back to a ballad on the London earthquake of 1580 - and even earlier to a continental European origin.

The dance is in a common 18th century form, a longways duple improper - the staple formation of modern New England contra dancing. If you slide smoothly from the swing into holding hands four-in-line you can enjoy an uplifting sense of fellowship as you march down the hall singing the chorus.

N.B. For an easier version, stay in waist-shoulder hold with your neighour as you march down, wheel ½ about as a couple, and return in the same hold, only sliding into holding hands when back in long lines on the side. For a slightly more challenging version at the end instead of just facing across after returning back up have the 1s in the centre be assisted by the 2s on the outside into a mirror hand caste up and the long way around into progressed position in line.

17. Good King Wenceslas

♩ = 110 [A] ... [B]

C F C G F G C C G Am

Intro.

F G C C F G Am G Em F G Am F C F C

Form square sets of 4 couples numbered acw with 5ᵗʰ couple in the middle facing 1s. **Start** l.f.. **Prepare** for brisk walking and slip circling. **Finish sequence** with former 1s ready to start from the middle, and the 5s from the middle ready to start as 4s, 4s become 3s, 3s become 2s, and 2s become 1s (essentially a one place cw progression**). Play and dance** the 18-bar sequence **5 times** through for all to dance from every position and return home.

Good King Wenceslas looked out
On the Feast of Stephen,
When the snow lay round about,
Deep and crisp and even;
Brightly shone the moon that night,
Tho' the frost was cruel,
When a poor man came in sight,
Gath'ring winter fu-u-el.

'Hither, page, and stand by me,
If thou know'st it, telling,
Yonder peasant, who is he?
Where and what his dwelling?'
'Sire, he lives a good league hence,
Underneath the mountain;
Right against the forest fence,
By Saint Agnes' fountain.'

'Bring me flesh, and bring me wine,
Bring me pine logs hither;
Thou and I will see him dine,
When we bear them thither.'
Page and monarch, forth they went,
Forth they went together,
Through the rude wind's wild lament
And the bitter weather.

'Sire, the night is darker now,
And the wind blows stronger;
Fails my heart, I know not how,
I can go no longer.'
'Mark my footsteps, good my page;
Tread thou in them boldly;
Thou shalt find the winter's rage
Freeze thy blood less coldly.'

In his master's steps he trod,
Where the snow lay dinted;
Heat was in the very sod
Which the saint had printed.
Therefore, Christian men, be sure,
Wealth or rank possessing,
Ye who now will bless the poor,
Shall yourselves find blessing.

A1 Waves up and down, starting 1s under 5s and into centre, over 3s and out, and continuing with simple solo turning about at ends.

A2 Continue waves till all back in place then 5s and 1s take 4hs at top of set.

B With 8 slip steps, 5s and 1s circle 1½ to change places and let go of other couples hs, leaving former 1s in the middle.
With 12 slip steps the 4 outside couples grand circle left 1¼ to finish one corner beyond original position.

This carol was written by John Mason Neale (1818-1866). Born in London, Neale studied and became a lecturer at the University in Cambridge. Later he studied for the priesthood but as a result of some radical views was not able to find a job as a priest and took up being a warden in Sackville College in East Grinstead, England. There he wrote many Christian songs, including this famous carol which he set a tune, 'Tempus Adest Floridum', in the then recently discovered 16ᵗʰ century Finnish carol book *Piae Cantiones*. This tune, the title of which translates as 'Spring has unwrapped her flowers' goes back to a 13ᵗʰ Century spring/Easter carol. The 'Good King Wenceslas' carol was first published in *Carols for Christmas Tide*, 1853, by John Neale and Thomas Helmore. The narrative may be confused and there may never have been a King Wenceslas, but there was an historic Bohemian Duke Vaclav (925-929), famed for his philanthropy. His father was Christian and mother pagan, and he was brought up by his Christian grandmother. Thought kind, even 'holy', by the people, he was murdered by his jealous pagan brother, Boleslav. Boleslav later repented, became a Christian and had Vaclav's remains enshrined in Prague.

With the good King looking down from his castle wall and with his name being borne by a famous square in Prague, this dance had to be in a quadrille formation. The fifth couple in the middle gives an opportunity for some dancers to look on while others labour up and down in the waves of snow. When it is your turn to enter the waves make sure you are not tempted to add any fancy turns to change side at the ends with your partner as there simply isn't time. 5 times through will get all back to place.

John Garden, *The Christmas Carol Dance Book*, December 2002

18. Gower Wassail

Form a tight circle of as many as will holding hs, own l.arm crossed over own r.arm, no partner necessary. **Start** l.f. **Prepare** for stomping triple steps (l, r, l and r,l,r) and mazurka hobble steps (l,r,hop and l,r,hop). **Finish** sequence having circled to left but without having released either hand or changed place. **Play** the 24 mazurka/waltz **and dance** sequence **as many times as will.**

A wassail, a wassail throughout all this town,

Our cup it is white and our ale it is brown.
Our Wassail is made of good ale and true,
Some nutmeg and ginger the best we could brew.
Fol the dol, fol the doldy dol, fol the doldy dol, fol the doldy dee,

Fol dai-rol lol the daddy, Sing too ral aye do!

A1 Turn out over l.sh., unlooping l.arm, with a l, r, l and point r.heel then turn back in over r.sh., relooping l.arm over with a r, l, r and point l.heel.
Turn all the way over l.sh. and finish facing back in, this time r.arm looped over, with a l,r,l r,l,r l,r,l point r.heel.

A2 Repeat all above until back in starting position, but starting with opposite foot, over opposite shoulder and pointing opposite foot.

B With own l.arm crossed over own r.arm and leaning out take 4 mazurka hobble steps (step onto l.f., bring r.f. up to it and take weight, then hop on r.f.) to turn the basket to left.

C All go in with 2 bourrée steps (6 stomping running steps) and out with 2 bourrée steps (6 running steps).

Our wassail is made with an elderberry bough, / And so my good neighbour we'll drink unto thou. / Besides all the earth, you'll have apples in store / Pray let us come in for it's cold by the door.
- *Chorus -*

We hope that your apple trees prosper and bear / So we may have cider when we call next year, / And where you've one barrel I hope you'll have ten / So we can have cider when we call again.
- *Chorus -*

There's master and mistress sit down by the fire / While we poor wassailers do wait in the mire, / So you pretty maid with your silverheaded pin, / Please open the door and let us come in.
- *Chorus -*

Here's we jolly wassail boys growing weary and cold, / Drop a small bit of silver into our old bowl, / And if we're alive for another New Year / Perhaps we may call and see who do live here.
- *Chorus -*

A tune and lyric collected from the singing of Phil Tanner, who died in a workhouse in South Wales in 1947.

To help support the overindulging waissailers in this carol, here is a dance which can be performed without ever letting go of the hands of your neighbours in the circle. The same was the case in the dance for 'The Angel Gabriel from Heaven came', but whereas that dance required partners and was gentle and hypnotic, this one does not need a partner and is in a bouncy triple-time. The dance matches the lyric to the extent that the raising of hands to turn this way mimes the carolers raising their mugs to receive, toast or drink, and the basketing left with the 'lopsided' hobble mazurka steps mimes the results of drinking too much.

19. Hail Happy Morn

Form longways proper sets of 7 couples. **Start** M l.f. W r.f.. **Prepare** for walking and slip steps. **Finish sequence** with same partner, the top 4 couples having progressed to the bottom. **Play and dance** sequence **7 times** through.

Hail, Hail,	Intro	All <u>forward with 2 slow steps</u> (M l and r, W r and l).
Hail happy morn thrice happy	A1	With 6 steps <u>1s 2h turn</u> each other ½ way (finishing facing each other from other side arms wide) *while* <u>everyone else cast</u> over top shoulder (M's l., W's r.) nearly all the way to <u>back to place</u>.
we/Hail happy morn thrice happy we,	A2	As everyone else takes a 7th step (on the final 'we') back into place, <u>1s begin</u> (on the overlapping 'Hail') to take <u>4 face-to-face galop steps down</u> then, releasing front hs, swing joined hs (M's r W's l) forward for <u>another 4 galop steps back-to-back</u> to bottom of set.
Who from our bondage are set free.	B	1M with 7W and 1W with 7M <u>galop back up set</u> but <u>1s turn in on 5th galop step to face each other</u> and on last 3 steps <u>1M take hs with 7M over 1W taking hs with 7W</u>.
From Jesse's side doth spring a ray,	C	<u>'Knot-of-4'</u> take 8 slip steps <u>down to bottom of set</u> then <u>release trailing hs so outside</u> dancers can <u>take hs with own side bottom person</u> (7W with 6W, 7M with 6W) <u>and inside people</u> can <u>swing out into line</u> (1W under M's arms then 1M to beside 7M).
And turn our darkesome nights to day.		<u>Lines-of-3 galop back up</u> just past the top of set and collect top person (2M&W) on bottom of line.
Sweet hallelujah let us sing	D1	<u>Lines-of-4 galop back down</u> just past bottom of set and collect bottom
Sweet hallelujah let us sing		person (5M&W) on top of line.
To God our Saviour		<u>Lines-of-5 galop back up</u> inside just past the top of set and collect top
And our King.		person.
Sweet hallelujah let us sing	D2	<u>Lines-of-6 galop down</u> inside just past the bottom of set.
Sweet hallelujah let us sing		
To God our Saviour		<u>Lines-of-7</u> galop back <u>galop back up</u>.
And our King.		

Hail mighty Prince eternal King
Let heaven and earth rejoice and sing
Angels and men with one accord
Break forth in songs to praise the Lord.
- *Chorus* -

Hark a glad voice the sinner cheers -
Prepare a way, a God appears.
The dumb doth speak, the dead are raised;
The lame doth walk and sing his praise!
- *Chorus* -

This carol is part of a multiple-part repertoire known as 'West Gallery Music'. After the Restoration, efforts to improve the music of regular church services included the erection of a gallery for singers and musicians at the west end of churches. The choirs and bands which developed soon became central to the social fabric of villages, as described by Thomas Hardy in his *Under the Greenwood Tree*. Hardy was himself a third-generation member of such a choir band and it is from manuscripts formerly belonging to the Hardy family, brought to light by Dave Townsend that this carol comes. To capture the fugueing of the manuscripts opening bars, number 1 couple must be alert as to when to start their first galop down the centre. So as to not loose time in the middle of the B part between unravelling from the 'Knot-of-4' and returning in 2 facing lines-of-3, outside people should be prepared to promptly release trailing hand and offer it to the same neighbour with whom they had started the sequence, and inside people should be prepared to swing out quickly (first W than M). If necessary, the lines-of-3 can straighten out as they return up the set.

John Garden, *The Christmas Carol Dance Book*, December 2002

20. Hanacpachap cussicuinin

Form couples facing along the l.o.d., holding candles at shoulder height in both hands, arms raised and wide so W's left forearm crosses over (and perhaps rests on) man's right forearm. **Start** left foot. **Prepare for** stately walking. **Play and dance** the sequence **as many times as will**.

	Quechua	English	
A	Hanacpachap cussicuinin, Huaran cacta muchas caiqui.	Heaven's joy! a thousand times shall we praise you.	Promenade forward with slow left-and-quick right-left-right-left (*count* 1 and 1-2-3-4) counterpart slow right-and-quick left-right-left-right and on last step swivel to face partner arms wide unlinked.
B	Yupairuru pucocmallqui, Runa cunap suyacuinin.	O tree bearing thrice-blessed fruit, O hope of humankind,	Honour partner with sideways step-left-and-bow sideways step-right-and-bow, ending with swivel to link raised right fore-arms
C	Callpannacpa quemicuinin,	helper of the weak.	Turn partner cw with pattern of A footwork, ending swivelling about to linked raised left forearms, then turn partner acw, ending releasing arms to face
D	Huaciascaita.	hear our prayer!	With timing of B both take slow step left, then turn single over r.sh. with 5 steps: r-l-r-l-r.
	Second verse		
	Uyarihuai muchascaita Diospa rampan Diospamaman Yurac tocto hamancaiman Yupascalla, collpascaita Huahuaiquiman suyuscaita Ricuchillai.	Attend to our pleas, O column of ivory, Mother of God! Beautiful iris, yellow and white, receive this song we offer you; come to our assistance, show us the fruit of your womb.	N.B. If not progressing, end take promenade hold with same partner. If progressing, end man having progressed on to new partner, man along woman against l.o.d.

This **hymn** appeared for the first time in Juan Pérez Bocanegra's *Ritual, formulario, e institución de curas para administrar a los naturales de este reyno, los santos sacramentos del baptismo, confirmacion, eucaristia, y viatico, penitencia, extremauncion, y matrimonio*, Lima, Geronymo de Contreras, 1631. Bocanegra was a Francisan friar and wrote most of the book in both Quechua and Spanish. This hymn was offered in the Quechua language without translation. The music is arranged in four parts with the *tiple* and *tenor* on pages 708 and the *alto* and *baxo* on p.709. The first verse is written underneath. The remaining verses follow on pages 710–712. Bocanegra claims to be responsible for the lyrics in his work but it is not clear if Bocanegra or an indigenous South American wrote the music. Immediately preceding the presentation of this hymn Bocanegra wrote on p.707 **La Oracion que se sigue en verîo Safico, en la lengua Quecha, hiz en loor de la Virgen fin manzilla: y va compue sta en musica a quarto vozes, para que la canten los cantores, en las processions, al entrar en la Igliesia, y en los dias de neustra Senora, y sus festiuidades** ('The hymn that follows is in Saphic verse and in the Quecha language, and is used in the procession of the Virgin, and in the days of our Lady, and its festivities, it is in four voices to be sung by singers in their procession and in entering church'). The referred to day falls on the 25 March. The rhythmic structure is unusual (being 3, 3, 4, 3, 3, 4), the harmonic structure is characteristic of Renaissance sacred music and the text, while being an ode to the Virgin Mary, contains many metaphors about love and nature that are grounded in Quecha culture.

I'm indebted to Charis Messalina Helena de Valence for introducing me to this carol and to *I Progetti*, the chamber choir she directs, for singing this for dance at our Christmas carol balls, and to match the music (and its original purpose) I wrote the following processional dance, for which each participant holds two candles. It proved magical. Depending on the nature of the occasion, the number of verses to be sung, the experience of the dancers and the space available you might want to do as we did, and use three or four times through the non-progressive form of the dance for some candle-holding dancers to process in under the gaze of others and then, when the column is bent around the dance space such that the first couple is behind the last couple, enjoy three or four times through the progressive form of the dance.

708   O R A C I O N E S

TIPLE.

Hanacpachapcuſſicuinin, huaracaɛta muchaſcaiqui.

Yupai rurupucoc mallqui, runacunap ſuyacuinin,

Callpannacpa quemicuinim, huac iaſcaita.

TENOR.

Hanacpachapcuſſicuinin, huarācaɛta muchaſcaiqui.

Yupai rurupucoc mallqui   runacunap ſuia.

cuinin, callpānacpa quemicuinin , huacyaſcaita.

709   DIVERSAS.

ALTO.

BAXO.

710   O R A C I O N E S

Vyarihuai muchaſcaita
Dioſpa rampan Dioſpa
    mamān
Yurac toɛto hamancai-
    mān
Yupaſcalla, collpaſcaita
Huahuaiquiman ſuyuſcai-
    ta
    Ricuchillai.
Chipchijcachac catachi-
    llai
Punchau puſſac quean tu-
    pa
Cam huacyacpac , mana-
    vpa
Queçaiquiɛta hamuiñillai
Piñalcaita queſpichillai
    Suſurhuana.
ñocahina pim huanana
Mitanmanta çananmanta
Teçҫe machup churinmā
    ta
Llapa yallec millaimana
Muchapuai yaſuihuana
    Huahuaiquiɛta.
Vequeɛta ricui pinquiɛta
çuҫu çucai huacachcacmā

ſonco queue putichcacmā
Cutirichij ñauıjquiɛta
Ricuchihuai vyayquiɛta
    Dioſpamaman.
Hanae pachap callaſanan
Canchac punchau tutaya-
    chec
Quilla pacſa raurayachec
Angelcunap cochocunan
Hinantimpa rirpucunan
    Cauҫac pucyu.
Capacmanta mirac ſuyu
Capaҫcunap capacnim-
    pa
ñaupamanta huachacnim
    pa.
Gracia ſococ, aclla puyu
Campim ſuyan tecce mu-
    yu
    Dioſcuſſichec.
Cori huātu Dioſpurichec
Huc ſimihuan huñiſpalla
Dios churiɛta chaipacha-
    lla
Vicçaiquipi runacachec
Vcuiquipi camacachec,
    Runapmarcan.
             Huaina

711   DIVERSAS.

Huaina huallpap cuſſip
    marcan
Pucarāmpa queſpi pun-
    cun
Ahuaſcaiquim , yupai vn-
    cun
Camtam alluecpac acllar-
    can
Quiquijquipitac munar-
    cán
    Runa caita.
Vſachipuai cauҫaita
Purum tazque hupaicui-
    hua
Dios çiҫac inquill huibua
Maimantañach ,, Acoyaita
Vſlachijman, cam mamai-
    ta
    Catachilla.
Canchác raurac, çuma qui
    lla
Checan punchaupa çecai-
    nin
Hinantimpa ſuyacuinin,
Cammillacpac choqueilla
Mana yauyac pápaquilla
    Dioſpallaɛtan.

Camman Coya? pillam pa
    ɛtan
Tucui ſanɛtocunamanta
Llapa Angelcunamanta
Cupaipa vmanta huaɛtan
Allpahuan tupuɛta raɛtan
    Sutillaiqui.
ñuc ñu ruruc chunta mall
    qui
Runacunap munai callcha
Pucai pucai çumacpallcha
Sutarpu tucuchec callqui
Titu huachec ñauillaiqui
    Queſpi huampu.
Cammicáqui Capac tápu
Mai maicamapas vyaylla
Catequeiquipac munailla
Hatú ſoncopas hairampu
Cumuicoccunapac llápu
    Huacchaicuya.
Vichcaicuſca cuſſi muya
Capac yayap camacuna
Yupai tica, acllacuna
Ieſus puricchec vruya
Pillco chátac cáchac cuya
    Suyacuncai.
çapallaiquin quemicuncái
    Zz 4   Can-

21. Hark the Herald Angels Sing

Form longways sets of 3 couples facing up and holding inside hs with partner. **Start** either foot. **Prepare for** walking and slip steps. **Finish each sequence** with tops at bottom of set, others one place up, ready for new introductory figure. **Play and dance** the 20-bar sequence **three times** for all to arrive home.

Hark! the herald angels sing:	A1	All 3 couples go <u>up a double</u> with stately r,l,r and close
'Glory to the newborn King!'		and back a double with l,r,l and close.
Peace on earth, and mercy mild,	A2	<u>Repeat</u> A1.
God and sinners reconciled.'		
Joyful, all ye nations, rise,	B1	<u>1M change</u> by near hand (r.h.) <u>with 2W</u> and face across set.
Join the triumph of the skies;	B2	<u>1W change</u> by near hand (l.h.) <u>with 2M</u> and face across set.
With th' angelic host proclaim:	C	1s take 2hs and slip <u>between 3s</u> who slip up into middle place.
'Christ is born in Bethlehem.'		<u>1s 2h turn ½ way</u> at bottom *while* 2s do same at top of set.
Hark! the herald angels sing:	D	Taking hs in line, <u>all</u> fall <u>back</u> and
'Glory to the newborn King!'		then come <u>forward</u>.

Christ, by highest heav'n adored:	A-D	As above except in A part <u>side with partner</u> by r.sh. then l.sh.
Christ, the everlasting Lord;		
Late in time behold him come,		
Offspring of the favoured one.		
Veil'd in flesh, the Godhead see;		
Hail, th'incarnate Deity:		
Pleased, as man, with men to dwell,		
Jesus, our Emmanuel!		
- *Chorus* -		

Hail! the heav'n-born Prince of peace!	A-D	As above except in A part <u>arming</u> right then left <u>with partner</u>.
Hail! the Son of Righteousness!		
Light and life to all he brings,		
Risen with healing in his wings		
Mild he lays his glory by,		
Born that man no more may die:		
Born to raise the sons of earth,		
Born to give them second birth.		
- *Chorus* -		
- *Repeat Chorus* -	D2	Repeat D part of dance to end.

The prolific hymn-writer Charles Wesley included words similar to these in his 1739 *Hymns and Sacred Poems*. The original ten 4-line verses were turned into three 8-line verses once the hymn was wedded by the Essex organist William H. Cummings to the Felix Mendelssohn tune. This tune (which Mendelssohn was said to have thought too merry for sacred words) was part of a 1840 cantata honouring printer Johann Gutenberg on the 400th anniversary of the invention of printing. Cummings' setting of the carol was first published by Richard Chope in his 1857 *Congregational Hymn and Tune Book*. This dance is in the '1651 First edition Playford' style where the 3 parts begin with doubles, siding and arming. The B part is not dissimilar from that in Playford's 'Once I loved a Maiden Fair'.

22. Here We Come a Caroling

Form short chains of 3 dancers of any gender holding hs, person on left no.1. 1's r.h. holds 2's r.h. 2's l.h. holds 3's l.h. **Start** either foot. **Prepare for** walking and kicking. **Finish sequence** with lead dancer now at end (far right) of line, others having moved along one place. **Play and dance** the 7-bar jig 13-bar march sequence **as many times as will**.

Here we come a-caroling Among the leaves so green, Here we come a wand'ring, So fair to be seen. *Love and joy come to you,* *And to your wassail too* *And God bless you and send you* *a Happy New Year,* *And God send you* *a Happy New Year.*	**A** No 1, following own free l.h., <u>leads others 16 steps</u> off to left, going anywhere on dance floor, including under joined hands of members of other trios. **B** <u>Step</u> on one foot and <u>kick</u> other, <u>step</u> on other foot and <u>kick</u> first foot <u>Repeat</u>. **C** <u>Lead dancer chain to other end of set</u> by <u>turning</u> 2nd in line by <u>r.h. 1½ at top</u> of set Lead dancer turns 3rd in line <u>l.h. 1½ at bottom</u> of set. Finish with a new leader ready to follow their own left hand.

We are not daily beggars
Who beg from door to door,
But we are neighbour's children
Whom you have seen before.
- Chorus -

Good master and good mistress
While you're sitting by the fire,
Pray think of us poor children
Who are wandering in the mire.
- Chorus -

We have a little purse
Made of ratching leather skin;
We want some of your small change
To line it well within.
- Chorus -

Bring us out a table
And spread it with a cloth
Bring us out some mouldy cheese,
And some of your Christmas loaf.
- Chorus -

God bless the Master of this house,
Likewise the Mistress too;
And all the little children
That round the table go.
- Chorus -

And all your kin and kinfolk
That dwell both far and near
We wish a Merry Christmas
And Happy New Year.
- Chorus -

Here is a thoroughly secular traditional English carol, full of Christmas and New Year cheer and with no mention of the birth of Jesus. In medieval times wassailers (from 'waes' well-being and 'hael' greet) would go from door to door singing carols and wishing householders good health. In return they would expect a small gratuity, a penny, a pork pie or a sip from the householders' bowl of spiced ale. In the nineteenth century the term 'wassailer' gave way to the name 'waits', derived from the name of the watchmen who once sounded their horns or played a tune to mark the passing hours of the night, but the custom persisted. Though the text here recorded was first published around 1850, some lines go back to the 17th century.

As the song suggests, this is a dance for young and old, children and adults, and no partner is necessary. One way to form the necessary chains is to call on dancers to form random lines of 3 (or a 3-person wide upward-facing column), then ask the middles to about face. However, they form, the lines should be encouraged to begin by go in as many different directions as possible. The wandering around the dance floor in the first part of the dance can involve curling around other lines, even going through arches made by other lines, as long as all are in a clear straight line to start the second part of the dance. The chain in the C part of the dance can be somewhat dizzy and disorienting, but the lead dancer should simply keep focus on getting to the bottom of the set after wishing each of the other dancers well with a r.h. or l.h. turn. A new leader will emerge ready to follow their left hand.

Because no one starting foot will feel equally natural for every dancer in every position I recommend you not bother dancers with a mandated starting foot. There is room in B for the step-kicks to work irrespective of foot.

Option: In the C part of the dance the person who is not being turned, instead of simply remaining still might turn once about with 8 steps. To make this work the turn has to be precisely once about. 3s turn over r.sh. when the others are r.h. turning above, and 2s turn over l.sh. when the others are l.h. turning below.

23. The Holly and the Ivy

Form lines-of-3 of any gender facing along l.o.d., ends holding centre's near hand in their outside hand and other end's hand behind centre's back. **Start** either foot. **Prepare for** travelling bourrée or quick waltz steps (stomping running steps in triple time). **Finish the sequence** with centre people having progressed on along the l.o.d. to start dance between two new neighbours. **Play and dance** the 16-bar bourrée sequence **as many times as will**.

The holly and the ivy,
When they are both full grown,

Of all the trees that are in the wood,
The holly bears the crown.
The rising of the sun,
And the running of the deer,

The playing of the merry organ,

Sweet singing in the choir.

The holly bears a blossom
As white as any flower
And Mary bore sweet Jesus Christ
To be our sweet Savior.
- Chorus -

The holly bears a berry
As red as any blood
And Mary bore sweet Jesus Christ
To do poor sinners good.
- Chorus -

The holly bears a prickle
As sharp as any thorn
And Mary bore sweet Jesus Christ
On Christmas day in the morn.
- Chorus -

The holly bears a bark
As bitter as any gall
And Mary bore sweet Jesus Christ
For to redeem us all.
- Chorus -

The holly and the ivy,
When they are both full grown,
Of all the trees that are in the wood,
The holly bears the crown.
- Chorus -

A   Not letting go, <u>centre</u> reverses under others' joined arched hs and <u>goes</u> cw <u>round l.h. end</u> *while* ends turn back-to-back under own hs and then centre turns under own still raised r.h. back into place.
<u>Centre</u> person reverses under joined hs and <u>goes</u> acw <u>around r.h. end</u> *while* ends turn back-to-back, then turns under l.h. into place.

B   <u>Ends</u> go forward, turn in and <u>raise</u> joined <u>hs over centre</u>.
Ends <u>pull centre forward</u>, lower joined hs behind centre's back, continue to pull centre forward while releasing joined hs and <u>turning over</u> outside <u>sh</u> to face back against the l.o.d..
Ends give inside hs to new centre, turn in and join hs behind centres' back to <u>form new lines-of-3</u> that go forward and back along the l.o.d..
<u>All promenade forward</u>.

This carol was first found in a broadside published in Birmingham around 1710. 151 years later it was included in a *Christmas Carols* collection by Joshua Sylvester (thought to be a pseudonym used by William Sandys and William Husk). There have been many theories as to why this carol should feature holly and ivy. Some believe they are there to represent good for in medieval times it was mistletoe which was seen to have evil pagan associations and both holly and ivy were regarded as holy and shunned by witches. Some believe their pairing represents the battle of the sexes, for in many medieval lyrics holly stands for maleness and ivy for femaleness. Others suggest that they feature because they were two common Christmas decorations, being green in winter and easily collected from woodlands. Others suggest the holly features simply because its leaf and berry offer so many possibilities for illustrating the life and death of Christ. Whatever the reason, the carol's imagery clearly goes back a long way. The chorus has very medieval imagery, the expression 'merry organ' being found in Chaucer and the 'rising of the sun' having pre-Christian mid-winter solstice overtones.

This dance is ideal for when there is an imbalance between the number of men and women wanting to dance. The figure in the A part is drawn from a German/Austrian dance called the 'Spinnradl' or 'Spinning Wheel' but is used here to represent a holly bush struggling in a tangle of ivy. The B part echos the lyric. The ends raise their joined hs as if the rising sun, the centre is catapulted forward as if a startled deer, you reach out with your hands as if playing an organ and all advance in closely-knit straight line as if a choir singing.

24. Il est né, le divin Enfant

Form a circle of as many couples as will in inward-facing side-by-side back hold, r.hs joined behind W's back, l.hs behind M's back. **Start** M l.f., W r.f.. **Prepare for** travelling polka and heel-and-toe steps. **Finish sequence** having progressed 2 places, M against l.o.d., W along. **Play and dance** the 16-bar polka sequence **as many times as will, then finish with a repeat of the A part.**

Il est né, le divin enfant,	A	In back-hold <u>heel and toe with outside foot</u> (M's l.f., W's r.f.) <u>and</u> with one polka step in same hold, <u>twist about on own place to face out</u> of circle, then <u>heel and toe with other foot and</u> with one polka steps <u>switch back.</u>
Jouez haut-bois, resonnez musettes;		
Il est né, le divin enfant,		<u>Again heel, toe, twist, then heel, toe and</u>, letting go of joined r.h. <u>M retires towards centre facing out and W turns over l.sh. to face in, take r.hs with neighbour to form a star-like wave</u>, arms extended.
Chantons tous son avènement.		
Depuis plus de quatre mille ans	B	Releasing l.hs, pull past r.h. and <u>change places with neighbour on right</u> with 2 polka steps. Take l.hs with new neighbour.
Nous le promettaient les prophètes,		Releasing r.hs, pull past l.h. and <u>change with neighbour on left</u>.
Depuis plus de quatre mille ans		Releasing l.hs again pull past and <u>change with neighbour on right</u>.
Nous attendions cet heureux temps.		Releasing r.hs <u>M stays facing in while W on l.h. goes acw around M into back-hold on his r.side</u>, l.hs now behind his back, M slipping his r.h. under her l.arm to take her r.h. behind her back.

- Chorus -

Une étable est son logement,
Un peu de paille est sa couchette
Une étable est son logement,
Pour un Dieu quel a baisement.
- Chorus -

Ah! Qu'il est beau, qu'il est charmant,
Ah! Que ses grâces sont parfaites!
Ah! Qu'il est beau, qu'il est charmant,
Qu'il est doux, ce divin enfant!
- Chorus -

O Jésus, roi tout-puisant,
Tout petit enfant que vous êtes;
O Jésus, roi tout-puisant,
Régnez sur nous entièrement.
- Chorus -

The tune for this carol can be found in R. Grosjean's *Airs des noêl lorrain* (1862), where it is called 'Ancien air de chasse', and an old Normandy hunting tune 'Tête bizarde*'*, which though in 6/8, is indeed melodically very similar. *The Shorter New Oxford Book of Carols* editors suggest the tune is an 18th century composition in a rustic style. The text of this carol was first published in Dom G. Legeay's *Noêls anciens* (1875-6). An English version of the lyric in Geoffery Brace's *Carol for Carol Singers*, Cambridge University Press, 1991, goes:
Sing aloud the child is born, / This is a time for celebrating
Sing aloud the child is born / Now the day at last is here
We have waited four thousand years,
Now the day is at last upon us.
We have waited etc, / Now the day at last is here. / - Chorus -
In a stable poor he lay, / Only a manger for a cradle.
In a stable etc / Only a bed of straw and hay. / - Chorus -
Shepherd and kings from lands afar / Join the joyful celebration.
Shepherds and etc / Guided by the shining star. / - Chorus -
Such is the appeal this catchy tune, there is even a Mohawk version 'Rotonni Niio Roie Mia', collected from Harriet and Carol La France of the St Regis Mohawk reservation at Rogensburg in the U.S.

The A part of the dance uses a rustic heel-and-toe figure to pick up on the carol's 'celebration-in-a-rural-setting' imagery - the switching about in the side-by-side backhold still used today in some traditions (eg Latvian). The B part of the dance uses Christmas star imagery, and to make the star twinkle clearly dancers should change crisply when chaining and finishing each chain with straight arms. As the carol normally ends with the A part, dancers can finish unwrapping into a wave and bowing to neighbours.

25. In Dulci Jubilo

Form a double circle of as many couples as will, M on inside, W outside, facing along l.o.d. holding inside hs. **Start** l.f.. **Prepare for** doubles and singles, always starting on alternate feet. **Finish sequence** with M having progressed 2 places along the l.o.d. and W 2 places against the l.o.d.. **Play and dance** the 16-bar walking sequence **as many times as will**.

In dulci jubilo	**A1** Starting l.f. <u>double forward (l,r,l,together)</u>.
Let us our homage show:	**A2** Starting r.f. <u>double back and face</u> partner (r,l,r,together).
Our hearts delight in pleasure	**B1** Greet partner with <u>singles left and right</u>.
Lies in praesepio;	L.f. double <u>on l.diagonal</u> pass partner r.sh and turn over l.sh.
And like a bright star shineth	**B2** <u>Facing new opposite,</u> greet with <u>singles right and left</u>.
Matris in gremio2.58	With r.f. double <u>on r.diagonal</u> pass opp. l.sh. and turn about over r.sh
Alpha es et O!	**C** Take <u>2h</u> and cw <u>turn</u> new partner with l.f. double.
Alpha es et O!	With r.f. double <u>turn same</u> acw <u>back to original side</u>.

O Jesu parvule,
My heart is sore for Thee!
Hear me, I beseech Thee,
O puer optime;
My pray let it reach Thee!
O princeps gloriae.
Trahe me post te.
Trahe me post te.

This carol, in its original 1400 Leipzig manuscript form, was a mixture of Latin and medieval German (technically known as the macaronic style) and was said to have been taught by angels to German mystic Heinrich Suso, who then joined them in a dance of worship. English versions started appearing as early as the 16th century. The version given here is based on one made in 1837 by Robert Lucas de Pearsall, an English lawyer, musician and amateur archaeologist, who converted to Catholicism and spent the last 30 years of his life in Germany.

O patris caritas!
O Nati lenitas!
Deeply were we stained
Per nostra crimina:
But Thou for us has gained
Coelorum gaudia.
Qualis gloria!
Qualis gloria!

> Good Christian men, rejoice / With heart and soul and voice;
> Give ye heed to what we say; / Jesus Christ is born today!
> Ox and ass before him bow, / The is in the manger now;
> *Christ is born today! Christ is born today!*
> Good Christian men, rejoice, / With heart and soul and voice;
> Now ye hear of endless bliss, / Jesus Christ was born for this!
> He has op'ed the heav'nly door / And man is blessed evermore.
> - *Chorus* -
> Good Christian men, rejoice, / With heart and soul and voice;
> Now ye need not fear the grave; / Jesus Christ is born to save.
> Calls you one and calls you all, / To gain his everlasting hall.
> - *Chorus* -

Ubi sunt gaudia,
If that they be not there?
There are Angels singing
Nova cantica:
And there the bells are ringing
In Regis curia.
O that we were there!
O that we were there!

In this dance, to match the provenance of this carol, we have late 16th century almain footwork (varying combinations of single and double steps alternating starting foot) - as in the English Inns of Court dances. The figures in each dance sequence offer an opportunity to make a double progression. To reduce the risk of confusion in the double progression, the dance leader might point out before the dancing starts that the M will be progressing continually along the l.o.d. and W against the l.o.d. and might invite everyone to look to their left and wave at their future partners.

26. Infant Holy, Infant Lowly

Form a circle of as many couples as will holding hs. Start M l.f., W r.f.. **Prepare for** waltz steps and 'twists'/knee-swivels. **Finish sequence** having progressed one place, M cw (against l.o.d.) W acw (along l.o.d.). **Play and dance** the 16-bar waltz sequence **as many times as will**.

Infant holy, infant lowly, For his bed a cattle stall;	A1	With 3 waltz steps <u>balance to neighbour and partner, then take neighbour in a r.sh. close ballroom hold </u>and conclude with a <u>twist</u> (legs together, heels swivel one way - say to left - as knees bend, drop and point other way - say to the right - then straighten up abruptly).
Oxen lowing, little knowing Christ, the babe, is Lord of all.	A2	With 3 waltz step starting again M r.f., W l.f. <u>turn briskly as a couple</u> 1½ cw and <u>twist</u> (this time knees to the left, heels to the right), finish pointing joined hs, chests, noses forward along the l.o.d.
Swift are winging, angels singing, Noels ringing, tidings bringing: Christ the babe is Lord of all.	B	In the dramatic forward-facing arms-extended ballroom hold, starting outside foot <u>promenade forward</u> with 4 waltz steps.
	C1	With 1 waltz step starting M l.f. W r.f., couple <u>turn</u> ½ acw, <u>M wheeling back</u>, <u>and all twist</u> (knees to the right, heels to left).
Christ the babe is Lord of all.	C2	With 1 waltz step starting M r.f. W l.f., couple <u>turn</u> ¼ back cw, <u>W wheeling back, open out</u>, sliding <u>into</u> holding hs in an inward-facing <u>circle</u>, <u>and all twist</u> (knees to left, heels to right).

Flocks were sleeping, shepherds keeping
Vigil till the morning new
Saw the glory, heard the story,
Tidings of a gospel true.
Thus rejoicing, free from sorrow,
Praises voicing greet the morrow:
Christ the babe was born for you.

This carol is version of a traditional Polish carol 'W Zlobie Lezy'. There is an English version of this carol called 'Jesus Holy, Born so Lowly' but the translation given here was made and published by Edith Reed in December 1921, without the repeating of the last line. Though today the last line is most commonly repeated, as given here, if it is not the dance can still work if the couple open out back into a circle at the end of C1.

To give some Polish polish to the dance, the chest should be 'puffed-up' proudly, the arms extended as much as possible (especially when promenading or in circle), and the leg twists should be executed with a snap (as in the Polish dance Adas Kujawiak). If displaying the dance you might like to make sure you all alternate the starting foot of the waltzes and alternate the direction of your twists (if your last waltz step was onto l.f., your knee goes to right on twist, if last step r.f., knee goes to left). In a social setting, however, the direction doesn't matter, so long as the dancers all drop at the knee and straighten up in unison, and the overall carriage is dramatic. With dancers who can chain smartly, a double progression is possible by replacing the above C1&2 with the following:
C1. With 1 waltz step starting M l.f. W r.f. <u>M guides W</u> with his r.h. under <u>his raised l.h. to take hs </u>in outward-facing circle then all <u>twist</u> (knees to the right, heels to left).
C2. With 1 waltz step starting M r.f. W l.f. <u>turn as a couple with neighbour,</u> W going under M raised r.h. <u>to finish</u> in each others places <u>in a new</u> inward-facing <u>circle then twist</u> (knee to left heel to right).

27. In the Bleak Midwinter

Form circular sets of 5 couples, M on inside, W outside, facing acw around set holding inside hand with partner.
Start l.f.. **Prepare for** pavan steps throughout (combinations of 2 singles and a double - starting on alternate feet).
Finish sequence with W having progressed one place cw, M one place acw. **Play and dance** the 16-bar pavan sequence **5 times** for all to arrive back in original place with original partner.

In the bleak mid-winter
Frosty wind made moan,
Earth stood hard as iron,
Water like a stone;
Snow had fallen, snow on snow
Snow on snow,
In the bleak mid-winter,
Long ago.

A1   All promenade around set with <u>singles left and right</u> <u>and with a double left</u>.
A2   With a r.f. sequence <u>M goes cw ¾ around W</u> *while* W turns acw <u>under M's raised r.h.1¼</u> till both facing in.
B   Holding hs in circle, all take <u>singles</u> left and right <u>into centre,</u> All <u>retire with l.double</u>.
      With a r.f. sequence <u>W goes cw ¾ around</u> r.side <u>neighbouring M</u> *while* <u>M turns</u> acw <u>under W's raised r.h.</u> 1¼ <u>finishing M</u> back on inside <u>facing W</u> on outside, <u>changing hs</u> so W's l.h. is in M's r.h. <u>and opening out to face along</u> the l.o.d..

Our God, heaven cannot hold him
Nor earth sustain;
Heaven and earth shall flee away
When he comes to reign;
In the bleak mid-winter
A stable place sufficed
The Lord God almighty
Jesus Christ.

Enough for him, whom cherubim
Worship night and day.
A breastful of milk
And a mangerful of hay;
Enough for him, whom angels
Fall down before,
The ox and ass and camel
Which adore.

Angels and archangels
May have gathered there,
Cherubim and seraphim
Thronged in the air:
But only his mother / In her maiden bliss
Worshipped the beloved
With a kiss.

What can I give him, / Poor as I am?
If I were a shepherd
I would bring a lamb;
If I were a wise man
I would do my part;
Yet what I can I give him
Give my heart.

Although Christmas was linked by the 4th century church with 25th December as part of a strategy to Christianise various winter solstice pagan festivals, there is no biblical association of the birth of Jesus with mid-winter. Poetry has, however, been found in the notion that mankind's greatest hope was born in the bleakest hour. This poem appeared, dated 1872, in the posthumous collection of Christina Rossetti, a deeply religious daughter of an Italian emigrée academic and English mother (so religious she refused the proposal of marriage from a man she loved deeply and thereafter became prone to melancholy). It was first used as a hymn in the *English Hymnal* of 1906, where it appeared with a tune composed by Gustav Holst, 'Cranham'. It is this magnificent moving tune which is given here.

Full pavan pattern footwork with final closures seems to not only suit the rhythm of this carol, but also to complement in mood the uplifting solemnity of this almost humanist lyric. At no stage during the dance is there a need to vary from the single-close, single-close, double-close footwork pattern characteristic of a pavan. Be sure to fill out the music fully by concluding each step, be it a single or a double, with a rising onto toes and settling down as you close. A certain balance is achieved in the choreography by having the M go cw around the W in the A2 then the W go cw around the M in the second half of the B part.

28. I Saw Three Ships

or in key of G

Form trios of any gender holding hs in lines anywhere on the dance floor. **Start** l.f.. Prepare for *chassé* or double steps throughout. **Finish sequence** with person from the r.h. end of one trio becoming the l.h. end of a new trio, and the person who was on the l.h. end of one trio becoming the middle person in the new trio. **Play and dance** the 8-bar jig sequence **as many times as will**.

I saw three ships come sailing in,
On Christmas Day, on Christmas Day.
I saw three ships come sailing in,
On Christmas Day in the morning.
And what was in those ships all three?
On Christmas Day, on Christmas Day,
And what was in those ships all three?
On Christmas Day in the morning.

A   In line-of-3, <u>double</u> (or *chassé*) <u>on left diagonal</u>. <u>Double on right diagonal</u>.

B   <u>Repeat</u> above <u>to face another trio and</u> ends can join raised hs to <u>form a circle</u>.

A   With 2 double steps <u>circle</u> 6 hs ½ way around, finishing with the former middles releasing r.h. to create 2 new trios.

B   <u>New middle</u> (formerly on left) <u>twists line about</u> by guiding person on their right (former middle) under the arch they have already raised with person formerly on the r.end of other line.

The Virgin Mary and Christ were there,
On Christmas Day, on Christmas Day.
The virgin Mary and Christ were there,
On Christmas Day in the morning.

Pray whither sailed those ships all three?
On Christmas Day, on Christmas Day,
Pray whither sailed those ships all three?
On Christmas Day in the morning.

O they sailed into Bethlehem,
On Christmas Day, on Christmas Day,
O they sailed into Bethlehem,
On Christmas Day in the morning.

And all the bells on earth shall ring,
On Christmas Day, on Christmas Day,
And all the bells on earth shall ring,
On Christmas Day in the morning.

And all the angels in heaven shall sing,
On Christmas Day, on Christmas Day,
And all the angels in heaven shall sing,
On Christmas Day in the morning.

Then let us all rejoice amain,
On Christmas Day, on Christmas Day,
Then let us all rejoice amain,
On Christmas Day in the morning.

This carol first appeared in appeared in William Sandys' 1833 *Christmas Carols, Ancient and Modern*. Its problematic text (you can't sail to Bethlehem) would seem to have its origins in the conflation of two medieval traditions. The first is that of increasingly elaborate stories about how, centuries after their death, the remains of the three wise men who visited the infant Jesus, were taken by boat to Constantinople, then to Milan and finally Cologne. The second is the 14th century German tradition of 'ship carols' in which Jesus' coming is compared in a mystical way to the arrival of a ship (indeed similar imagery has been found in a mid-16th century carol) and the number three was an echo of the Trinity. Less can be said about the tune. A rhythmic similarity has been noted between the text and the song 'There lived a man in Babylon' sung by Sir Toby Belch in Shakespeare's *Twelfth Night*. The modern-day tune is based on that Sandys' published in 1833, and the famous folk collector Cecil Sharp noted that it is not only also the tune of several 20th century secular folk songs - but also of an 18th century song 'As I sat on a sunny bank'.

In the A part of this dance dancers can glide forward like three proud ships first on one tack then on another - following the lead of the left most dancer, who is on the look out for another trio to circle up with (remembering that you increase your chances of randomly meeting another trio by not drifting too far to the outskirts of the dance floor). In the B part of the dance a new trios is created out of the former right end person of one trio and former left and middle person of another.

N.B. A simpler non-progressive version of the dance is possible by having the same middle person in each line doing the guiding and arching to twist the line about and the same left end person doing the leading.

29. It Came upon a Midnight Clear (1)

♩ = 160 [A]

3/4

Am   G⁷   C   F   Dm   G⁷   C |1.   G   C⁷   F |2

[B]

A   Dm   F   G   G⁷   C   Am   G⁷   C   F   Dm   C⁷   F   [Intro.]

Form as many couples-facing-couples as will, either in a Sicilian circle or randomly around the floor. **Start** l.f.. **Prepare for** travelling waltz steps. **Finish sequence** having progressed as a couple on to face a new couple. **Play and dance** the 32-bar waltz sequence **as many times as will**.

It came upon the midnight clear,
That glorious song of old,
From angels bending near the earth

To touch their harps of gold:

'Peace on the earth, good will to men,
From heaven's all-gracious King!'
The world in solemn stillness lay
To hear the angels sing.

Still thru the cloven skies they come
With peaceful wings unfurled;
And still their heavenly music floats
All o'er the weary world;
Above its sad and lowly plains
They bend on hovering wing.
And ever o'er its Babel sounds
The blessed angels sing.

Yet with the woes of sin and strife
The world hath suffered long;
Beneath the angel-strain have rolled
Two thousand years of wrong;
And man, at war with man, hears not
The love-song which they bring;
O hush the noise, ye men of strife,
And hear the angels sing.

And ye, beneath life's crushing load,
Whose forms are bending low,
Who toil along the climbing way
With painful steps and slow,
Look, now For glad and golden hours
Come swiftly on the wing:
O rest beside the weary road
And hear the angels sing.

For lo! the days are hastening on,
By prophet bards foretold,
When, with the ever-circling years,
Shall come the Age of Gold;
When peace shall over all the earth
Its ancient splendours fling,
And all the world give back the song
Which now the angels sing.

A1   With 4 waltz steps r.h. star with opposite couple.
     With 4 waltz steps r.sh. gypsy opposite, take 2h open hold.

A2   M raises l.arm, turns W cw over her r.sh., M lowers his r.arm behind her back and they wheel once about.
     M, letting go with r.h., goes under her r.arm to swap places then, with W going to right under M's raised l.h., swap back.

B   Holding hs in circle balance in and out then W r.h. chain across set
     With 4 waltz step turn opposite l.h. around till M facing in
     M r.h. chain across to partner, turning her l.h., joining r.hs over l.
     In skater's hold wheel or promenade to face new opposite.

This hymn was penned in the late 1840s by Edmund Hamilton Sears, a Unitarian minister in Massachusetts, reportedly at the request of his friend, W. P. Lunt, a minister in Quincy, Massachusetts. It was first sung at the 1849 Sunday School Christmas celebration and was published in Boston's Christian Register in 1850. It first appeared in Britain in 1870 when Edward Bickersteth included it in his *Hymnal Companion to the Book of Common Prayer,* rewording the 5th verse to remove the 'unbiblical' 'humanist' reference to a coming 'age of gold'. In the U.S. the carol is usually sung to the tune give above. This tune was written for the organ in 1850 by Richard Storrs Willis, then rearranged as a hymn by Uzziah Christopher Burnap. In Britain the carol is more commonly sung to a version of a traditional air, given on the next page to go with a dance in 4/4.

This longer-than-average-carol is of a very common dance-tune length and structure - 32 bars, A1&2 then B1&2. Accordingly it supports well this full-figured country style waltz sequence. I recommend a Sicilian circle formation - that is, couple facing one couple, with backs to another couple, all around the room. This formation is best suited to a big group in a big space, but if you do indeed have a big double circle and only sing the 5 standard verses to the carol, don't expect to progress all the way around back to where you began the dance - just enjoy the dance with your partner and five different opposite couples and then, if you wish, call for the carol and dance again. If danced as a Sicilian circle, the distance to promenade on to face a new opposite couple at the end of the sequence may not be very far, so in this situation you may simply wheeling on spot (M back, W forward). If danced as random couples on the floor, the distance to promenade on may be considerable, so no time should be lost taking skater's hold with partner, be straight away on the look out for potential opposites, and if there is not readily apparent head towards the centre of the dance floor (this will increase your chances of meeting another free couple).

30. It Came upon a Midnight Clear (2)

Form longways proper duple minor sets of as many couples as will. **Start** either foot. **Prepare for** walking steps. **Finish sequence** having progressed as couple one place up or down. **Play and dance** the 32-bar sequence **as many times as will.**

It came upon the midnight clear,

That glorious song of old,
From angels bending near the earth

To touch their harps of gold:
'Peace on the earth, good will to men,
From heaven's all-gracious King!'
The world in solemn stillness lay

To hear the angels sing.

*... and other verses as presented
on opposite page under
It Came Upon a Midnight Clear 1*

A   1M and 2W change places the long way by taking steps round outside of (passing l.sh. with) neighbour (M down W up).
1M and 2W l.sh. gypsy once around in middle of minor set.
1M and 2W 2h turn cw (back other way) once round then fall back (in same exchanged places) into hs four with neighbours.
All circle cw once around.

B   1W and 2M go round neigh. (W down, M up) to change places.
1W and 2M r.sh. gypsy once around.
2M and 1W 2h turn acw once around back the other way then (in same exchanged places) slip into hs four.
All circle acw ½ way round to original place then pull past up or down by l.sh, 1M & 2W ready to continue into new sequence.

As mentioned in the previous entry, this hymn was penned in America in the late 1840s by the Edmund Hamilton Sears, and in 1850 a fellow American, Richard Storrs Willis, wrote the triple time tune given on the previous page and to which it is still most commonly set in the U.S. The carol soon found its way to Britain where, in 1871, Arthur Sullivan gave it a new setting - matching it to the traditional tune given above which he called 'Noel'.

This dance well suits this double time version of this carol, individuals drifting like heavenly bodies in closing orbits towards their opposites, touching each other like angels, then falling back into circles like worshipping mortals. The B part of the dance is the mirror image of the A part, with the exception of the final progression up or down the set. To have the dance work well it is helps if dancers can keep their eyes on their corners for virtually the entire sequence – form the long orbit around neighbour into exchanged places through to the pulling of all into a circle (the circles always going the same way as the couple were 2h turning – that is to the left in the A part and to the right in the B part). Fixing eyes on each other will not only help synchronise the 'covering' of each other, but also help the first corners know when they stop dancing and the 2nds corners know when they start. It also helps if dancers appreciate that once they have changed places with their opposite, they keep returning to this exchanged position (facing against their original direction) until the final half circle right sets them facing again in original direction. The final pull through by the l.sh. gives the 1M and 2W the momentum and trajectory to start their orbit with their corners in the next minor set. The dance can be done to any 32 bar walking tune and, if not being done in a Christmas context to this tune, might become a contra called 'Heavenly Bodies' (the name by which I first called the sequence).

31. I Wonder as I Wander

Form as many couples as will facing along the l.o.d. holding inside hs. **Start** outside foot (M's l.f., W's r.f.). **Prepare for** travelling waltz steps. **Finish sequence** either staying with same partner or having progressed to a new, M against l.o.d, W along. **Play and dance** the 16-bar waltz sequence as many times as will.

I wonder as I wander out under the sky	A1	With 4 travelling waltz steps <u>M pass W across to left</u>, (from his r.h. to his l.h.) taking new inside hand.
How Jesus the Savior did come for to die	A2	<u>M pass W back to r.side</u>, and as she comes in front of M she puts her l.h. on her r.hip <u>and he puts his r.arm</u> (under joined arms) <u>behind her back</u> to take her l.h., <u>to flow into a</u> cw <u>wheel</u>, finishing M on inside facing along l.o.d., W on outside facing against..
For poor orn'ry people	B1	With 2 waltz steps <u>W</u> releases M's l.h. from her r.h. and <u>turns out over l.sh.</u> all the way to face back against l.o.d., her l.h. now holding M's r.h. in front of her chest, <u>and her r.h. slips behind the M's back</u> to take the l.h. which the M has put behind his l.hip.
like you and like I,		<u>M, doing as W did</u>, lets go with his r.h. to turn out over l.sh. once around, and resume back hold by slipping his r.h. back behind W's back to there once again take her l.h.
I wonder as I wander	B2	<u>W does a second turn out</u> over her l.sh. but this time <u>finishing facing partner</u> and hesitating with the music
out under the sky.		*Either,* <u>2h turn once around cw</u> and open out ready to start again with same partner, *Or,* <u>M guides W on</u> along l.o.d. <u>to next M</u> and reaches back against l.o.d. to receive own new partner.

When Mary birthed Jesus,
'twas in a cow's stall,
With wise men and farmers
and shepherds and all.
But high from God's heaven,
a star's light did fall,
And the promise of ages
it then did recall.

If Jesus had wanted / for any wee thing,
A star in the sky / or a bird on a wing.
Or all of God's angels / in heaven to sing, / He surely could have had it, 'Cause He was the King.

I wonder as I wander / out under the sky, / How Jesus the Savior / did come for to die. / For poor on'ry people like you and like I, / I wonder as I wander / out under the sky.

I Wonder As Wander
John Jacob Niles
Reproduced by Permission of Warner/Chappell Music Australia Pty.Ltd.
Unauthorised Reproduction is Illegal.

This carol was collected in Murphy, North Carolina in July 1933 by John Jacob Niles (1892-1980), a leading American folksong collector, who, it is said, paid a young travelling evangelist Annie Morgan 25c an hour to sing it until he had memorised it. Niles published it in his 1934 *Songs of the Hill-Folk*. It is often referred to as a traditional Appalachian carol, but just how far back it goes is not clear. Some believe it was only a generation old when collected. Its questioning pensiveness and gentle free speech lilt give it, nevertheless, a certain timeless quality.

To match the A part of this 'open air' carol is a very expansive almost wandering figure. Worked into the B part is the central feature of the beautiful waltz Lloyd Shaw learnt from a young Russian immigrant to the U.S. and included as 'The Tamara Waltz' in his 1948 classic *The Round Dance Book*. The hesitation towards the end of the tune is matched in the dance by a hesitation before taking 2hs with partner and turning or progressing on to a new partner. The dance leader may wish to make a game of switching between the two possible versions - at the hesitation inviting dancers to say 'hello' and stay with partner or say 'good-bye' and progress on. To make the face-to-face hesitation even more dramatic, make sure all the preceding figures are danced strictly side-by-side, promenading in A1 both facing forward, and starting and finishing the wheel in A2 and turns in B1 facing in exactly the opposite direction, r.sh. to r.sh.. Once mastered dancers will discover they can actually dance the turn outs in the B part while continuing to wheel.

32. Jesus Born in Bethn'y

Form a closed Beckett formation contra set with lines of couples facing across a contra set and with a couple at each end of the set. Start with either foot. Prepare for walking. Finish sequence with same partner having progressed 1 couples' place acw around set. There will be a new couple at the ends of the set, and all the other couples will be facing new opposites (having skipped one possible opposite couple- ie, a double progression). Play and dance the 32 bar reel sequence as many times as will.

Jesus born in Beth'ny,
Jesus born in Beth'ny
Jesus born in Beth'ny
And in a manger lay
- Repeat above -

A1   All go <u>forward and back</u> with 8 steps.

     <u>Dsd opposite</u> across the line of the set with 8 steps.

A2   <u>R.hs across with opposites ¾ of way</u>, from about ½ around starting to look up or down the column and reach out with l.h. <u>Lhs across with couple above or below</u> and once around.

In a manger lay,
In a manger lay
Jesus born in Beth'ny
And in a manger lay
- Repeat above -

B1   <u>R.sh. dsd the same opposite</u> as you dsd before but this time up-and-down the line of the set.
Take 4 hs and <u>circle</u> once around.

B2   M <u>swings</u> same <u>opposite</u> W in a ballroom hold on M's side of set, opening out with W on M's r.h. side facing across set.
<u>W chain across</u> to partner, who sweeps them into a <u>courtesy turn</u> (preferably in waist-shoulder hold) <u>and progresses</u> them <u>one</u> couples <u>place</u> acw around the set.

Jesus went a preachin' the Gospel of his God *etc.*

Judas did betray him and sold him for coin *etc.*

People crucified him and nailed him to the tree *etc.*

Joseph begged his body and placed it in a tomb *etc.*

Tomb it would not hold him he burst the bonds of death *etc.*

Early, then one morning, before the break of day *etc.*

Mary came a-weeping, 'They've stole my Lord away' *etc.*

Jesus has arisen and gone to Galilee *etc.*

Jesus then ascended up to his father's home *etc.*

This carol was included by John Jacob Niles, collector of 'I wonder as I wander', in *Ten Christmas Carols from the Southern Appalacian Mountains*, 1932. Though often sung in an AB format, it is commonly played instrumentally AABB - for example by the Baltimore Consort on their *A Bright Star Day* CD, where the tune is called 'A Christmas Jig'. For this dance the AABB structure is needed. Singers can either repeat every verse or leave the repeat to the instruments.

This jazzy tune is matched with an American style contra dance in the Beckett formation of couples standing beside their partner on one side or another of a column. In each sequence there are effectively three meetings with the same opposite (a holy trinity allusion?). The first is doing the do-si-do across the set, the second is doing the do-si-do up-and-down the set and the third is doing the swing. Accordingly, if dancers take note of their opposite on their first encounter and keep simply returning to them, the dance will flow easily. The dance can be done to any 64 beat walking tune, and if being danced in a non-Christmas context might take the name 'Triple Tryst' in honour of the 3 assignations you manage with each successive opposite.

Variant: It is possible to do this same dance in two large concentric but facing circles, partner beside you in the same circle facing another couple in the other circle. In this formation there is no need to have anyone resting on the ends, and, at the end of the sequence you wheel on only as far is necessary to face off with the next couple in the contrary circle.

John Garden, *The Christmas Carol Dance Book*, December 2002

33. Jingle Bells

Sheet music: ♩ = 120, key signature 4/4. Sections A and B with chords C, F, G7, C, F, G, C G (first line) and C, F, C, D7, G, G7, C (second line), with markings [A], [1.], [2], [B], Intro., [1.], [2].

Form a circle of as many couples as will, M facing along l.o.d., W against. **Start** l.f.. **Prepare for** travelling polka steps and heel and toe step. **Finish sequence** W having progressed one place along the l.o.d., M one place against the l.o.d. **Play and dance** the 32-bar polka sequence **as many times as will**.

Dashing through the snow
On a one-horse open sleigh
O'er the fields we go
Laughing all the way;

Bells on bob-tail ring
making spirits bright
What fun it is to ride and sing
A sleighing song tonight
Jingle bells, jingle bells
jingle all the way!
O what fun it is to ride
In a one-horse open sleigh, hey!
Jingle bells, jingle bells
jingle all the way!
O what fun it is to ride
In a one-horse open sleigh.

(Non official second verse)

Christmas time is here
And we all go to bed
As we climb the stairs
We nod our sleepy heads
We take our stockings off
And hang them in a row
And then jump quickly into bed
And off to sleep we go
- *Chorus* –

A1   Chain, 2 polka step for each hand, starting r.h. to partner,
l.h. to next
r.h. to next
then l.h. turn next about (r.h. in the air) till facing in opposite direction.

A2   Chain back same way, r.h.
l.h.
r.h. past original partner,
then l.h. to new partner, r.h. over top into skaters hold.

B1   Side-by-side and both facing along l.o.d., l.f. heel and toe twice.
4 quick galop steps on left diagonal, lift and turn r.sh. forward.
R.f. heel and toe twice and take 4 quick galop steps on r. diagonal, finishing raising hs to over sh. hold.

B2   Repeat above in high promenade hold with W in front of M to heel and toe, not side-by-side but in parallel, and finish releasing l.hs, facing original direction, ready to pull past by r.sh..

Though now almost synonymous with a jolly Christmas, this carol was actually written for a Thanksgiving performance by Sunday schoolers at a Boston church. James Pierpont, the Sunday school teacher, called his song 'The One Horse Open Sleigh' and the children's performance was so well received they were asked to repeat it at Christmas. The song has remained attached to Christmas ever since.

With bells on your toes, get ready to galop (or, to be more precisely, polka) a swerving path through a field of imaginary snow. Try to give your set a lot of space so two polka steps don't bring you too quickly to the next hand in the chain, but if the set is tight compensate by making wide ½ way turns (with eye contact) for each hand. Don't miss the opportunity to raise your r.h. when, laughing all the way, you turn the last person all the way about. After chaining back to and one place beyond your original partner turn the easy way into a low skater's hold for your first prancing promenade. At the end of B1 be sure not to miss the opportunity to give a loud 'hey' as you raise your hs, M's r.arm going over W's head, into a shoulder-high promenade hold. At the end of the sequence, as you turn out of the high promenade and release l.hs ready to chain on the r.h., don't forget the eye contact and a word of good-bye.

34. Joy to the World

Form an improper duple minor contra set or a Sicilian circle of as many couples-facing-couples as will. **Start** either foot. **Prepare for** both stately slow steps and brisk walking steps. **Finish sequence** having progressed as a couple one place in original direction ready to start sequence with new opposite couple (if in contra formation, when a couple 'pops' out the end of set they rest one turn before dancing back in other direction). **Play and dance** the 20-bar walking sequence **as many times as will**.

Joy to the world! The Lord is come
Let earth receive her King!

Let ev'ry heart
prepare him room,
And heaven and nature sing!
And heaven and nature sing!
And heaven and heaven
and nature sing!

A Give r.hs across and with 8 slow steps star nearly once around with opposites, W letting opposite M (1M 2W, 2M 1W) catch them up into high promenade hold.

B With 8 normal steps couples head up or down (1M promenades 2W down set *while* 2M promenades 1W up) .

C Staying on own side switch direction and with 8 normal steps promenade other way back.

D L.hs across with original opposites to star with 8 normal steps nearly once around, then turn out to face original direction to give r.h. up or down to new opposite.

Joy to the earth! The Saviour reigns:
Let men their songs employ,
While fields and floods,
rocks, hills and plains
Repeat the sounding joy,
Repeat the sounding joy,
Repeat, repeat
the sounding joy.

No more let sins and sorrows grow
Nor thorns infest the ground.
He comes to make
His blessings flow
Far as the curse is found
Far as the curse is found
Far as, far as
the curse is found.

He rules the world with truth and grace,
And makes the nations prove
The glories of
His righteousness
And wonders of his love
And wonders of his love
And wonders, wonders
of his love.

This hymn was written by Isaac Watts, born into an Independent (ie Congregational Church family) in 1674. It is said that at the age of 15 he complained to his father that church hymns were boring and meaningless and, challenged by his father to do better, Watts wrote a new hymn every week for the next two years. By the end of his life he had written more than 600 and is remembered today as 'the father of English hymnody'. As with many of Watts' hymns, this one from 1719 is a Christianised version of a Psalm - in this case Psalm 98, 'The Psalms of David'. The verses were not set to music until nearly 100 years later, when, in the 1830s, the American composer and music educator Lowell Mason put them to a tune he ascribed to 'George Frederick Handel'. Watts and Handel had indeed known each other when they lived in London. For the next 100 years people believed the tune to be Handel's, it certainly having echoes of the Messiah choruses, but it is now thought to be Mason's own Handelian-influenced composition. The tune is named after the city of Antioch, Syria, where believers were, according to *Acts* 11:26, first called 'Christians'.

To match the triumphant feel of the opening line of each of this carol's verses, beginning the dance sequence each time with a very stately, half-pace 8 step star. Just as the carol then swings into a quicker mode for the remainder of each verse, so does the dance. For novice dancers it may be best to do this dance in Sicilian circle formation so that dancers don't have to change roles at end of a contra set and the 'original direction' in which dancers are facing at the beginning of the dance is the same for every sequence.

35. The Little Drummer Boy

Form a longways set of 4 couple, all facing up. **Start** either foot. **Prepare for** marching. **Finish sequence** with same partner. **Play and dance** the 24-bar march either **three times**, once finishing facing down, once following the 8s and finishing facing up and again following the 1s but this time finishing facing partner, **or play and dance** the sequence **four times** through, each time finishing with the lead couple arching to the bottom and all facing up to follow new leaders.

Come they told me, Pa rum pum pum pum - -,	A1	<u>As individuals caste down own side</u> with 8 steps. Take partner's inside hand <u>and</u>, with 8 steps, <u>lead up</u>.
A new born King to see, Pa rum pum pum pum - -,	A2	<u>As couples</u> 1s <u>down</u> M's side, 2s down W's side, 3s M's side etc, then take hs in lines of 4 <u>and lead up</u>.
Our finest gifts we bring, Pa rum pum pum pum - -,	B	<u>Lines-of-4</u> alternate between <u>caste</u> to left and right. Take hs in a single line-of-8 <u>and lead up</u>.
To lay before the king, Pa rumpapumpum, rumpapumpum, rum pa pum pum - -	C	<u>Line-of-8</u> advance with 8 steps then fold back till on a middle pivot 2 lines of 4 are back-to-back and 8W can give her r.h. to the r.h. of 1M, then break line at top (2W and 3M) and 2 halves caste out / fold down till they face and 2W and 3M can take hs), then all fall back into circle.
So, to honour Him, Pa rum pum pum pum	A3	<u>All circle left ½ way</u> till 1s are at the bottom. <u>1s break away and lead up</u> to top, <u>others following</u>.
When we come…	D	As couples arrive home they either <u>2h turn ½ or 1½</u> and prepare to do the dance following the other end of the column, <u>or the 1s retire arching to the bottom of set</u> over the others who lead up.

Little baby / Pa rum pum pum pum
I am a poor boy too
Pa rum pum pum pum
I have no gift to bring
Pa rum pum pum pum
That's fit to give our King
Pa rumpapumpum, rumpapumpum,
rum pa pum pum
Shall I play for you
Pa rum pum pum pum
On my drum.

Mary nodded / Pa rum pum pum pum
The ox and lamb kept time
Pa rum pum pum pum
I played my drum for Him
Pa rum pum pum pum
I played my best for Him
Pa rumpapumpum, rumpapumpum,
The he smiled at me
Pa rum pum pum pum
Me and my drum…m.

Little Drummer Boy
Katherine Dvis/Henry Onorati/Harry Simeone
Reproduced by Permission of Warner/Chappell Music Australia Pty.Ltd.
Unauthorised Reproduction is Illegal.

This carol, telling of the shepherd boy who makes his way to the manger but has nothing to offer the infant but his music, was written by choral conductor Harry Simeone in 1958, with Henry Onorati and Katherine Davis. The tune was taken from the Spanish song 'Tabolilleros'. The work was released by Simeone on a chorale album *Sing We Now of Christmas*. The work entered the US charts each December for the next five year, and in 1963 the original album was retitled *The Little Drummer Boy*. The Harry Simeone Chorale version was soon followed by many other versions and the carol became internationally popular.

To give everyone the opportunity to march to this tender carol, here is a dance in which dancers can wheel this way and that as if on a parade ground, advance 8-a-breast to lay gift before the king, fold lines this way and that with military precision, form a circle 'to honour him' and all lead back to place in time to recommence either facing a new way or with a new leader. There are indeed two options for repeating the sequence. If it is intended to simple sing or play 3 verses, then finish the first verse all facing down, have the 8s be the leaders for the second verse (dancing figures 'up-side down'), finish this verse facing back up on original side, then have the 1s leaders again for the 3rd verse - all finishing facing partner. If you are happy to hear the tune four times (singers returning to repeat the 1st verse), you can commence each time all facing up, but, instead of concluding each sequence with a 2h turn, have the lead dancer retire arching to the bottom over the others as they move up, thus giving each of the couples an opportunity to lead the dance. A lot of space is recommended for this 'grand march in a set'.

36. Masters in this Hall

Form an improper longways duple minor contra set for as many couples as will, 1M and 2W facing up, 1W and 2M down. **Start** either foot. **Prepare for** brisk walking steps. **Finish sequence** having progressed one place up or down set in original direction. **Play and dance** as 32 jig sequence (my preference, i.e. with A2) **as many times as will**.

Masters in this hall
Hear ye news today,
Brought from over seas
And ever you I pray.
- *Repeat verse* -*(optional)*

Noel, Noel, Noel
Noel sing we clear!
Holpen all the folk on earth
Born the Son of God so dear!
Noel, Noel,
Noel sing we loud
God to day hath poor folk raised and
cast a-down the proud.

Shepherd many on one
Sat among the sheep,
No man spake more word
Than they had been sleep:
- *Repeat verse* -
- *Chorus* -

Then to Bethl'em town
Went we two by two,
In a sorry place
We heard the oxen low:
- *Repeat verse* -
- *Chorus* -

Ox and ass Him know,
Kneeling on their knee,
Wonderous joy had I
This little babe to see.
- *Repeat verse* -
- *Chorus* -

This is Christ, the Lord,
Masters be ye glad!
Christmas is come in,
And no folk shall be sad!
- *Repeat verse* -
- *Chorus* -

A1 1M chase 2W cw down round 2M, 2W continuing round 1W to M's place, 1M cutting between 2M and 1W to 2W's place.
2W chase 1M cw round 2M, 1M continuing round 1W home, 2W cutting between 2M and 1W to original place.

A2 Taking r.hs across all set right and left then star cw ½ way.
Without relinquishing r.hs across, repeat setting and ½ star cw to arrive home.

B1 2M chase 1W cw up round 1M, 1W continues round 2W to 2M's place, 2M cutting between 1M and 2W to 1W's place.
1W chase 2M cw round 1M, 2M continues round 2W home, 1W cutting between 1M and 2W to original place.

B2 Taking r.hs across all set right then left then star ½ way.

Taking r.hs with partner, set right and left then ½ r.h. turn so 1M and 2W end up facing down and 2M and 1W up.

The tune for this carol has a long association with dance. It was originally French and included in Raoul-Augur Feuillet's 1703 *Recueil de contredanse* along with a longways proper dance, 'La Matelotte', which Feuillet had himself written to go with the tune. In 1710 John Essex published a translation of this work, *For the Further Improvement of Dancing*, in which the dance is given as 'The Female Saylor'. It is unclear, however, whether the tune entered English folk tradition at that point, or whether it was reintroduced latter - possibly by a certain Edmund Sedding who is said to have obtained it in the mid-19th century from a French organist. Whatever the case, sometime around 1860 William Morris put his carol 'Master in this Hall' to the tune. A hundred years later Pat Shaw had a look at Feuillet's dance as it appeared in John Essex's book and published a version in his 1965 *Six Simple Country Dances*.

The dance offered here is different from both Feuillet's original dance and Pat Shaw's revision. The longways improper formation was chosen to give all the men an opportunity to act as 'Masters in this Hall' towards each woman they meet, until the tables are turned on them. The dance is simple if dancers remember that all the action is clockwise, that the man always starts the chasing, that whoever is doing the chasing takes the short cut, and that the right hand needs to come up towards each double chase ready for the balance and star (if doing the full 32-bar version). Indeed, although the tune itself is intrinsically and historically 32 bars, if dancing to choristers singing the 24-bar version (with no repeats of the verse), then you can shorten the dance by omitting the balance and star figure in A2. If the chasing in A1 and B1 looks to challenging, then it can be replaced with a simple 16 step chase all the way around to home.

John Garden, *The Christmas Carol Dance Book*, December 2002

37. Merry Christmas

Form a Sicilian circle of as many couples as will in high promenade hold facing another couple (offset a little to left). **Start** l.f.. **Prepare** for schottische steps and step-hops. **Finish sequence** back in high promenade with partner after having greeted two other couples. **Play and dance** the 16-bar schottische sequence **as many times as will.**

Sun gleams bright, hearts are light,	A1	Take 2 schottische steps <u>forward to draw level</u> (r.shs near) <u>with opposite couple</u>, W in front of her partner.
Merry, merry Christmas.		Retaining partner's l.h. but releasing partner's r.h. <u>greet opposites</u> (same sex opposite then their partner) <u>with r.hs</u> (with each 1 beat to take hs, 1 beat to shake)
Bells ring out, children shout	A2	Release these opposites, <u>resume high promenade with partner, and</u> take 2 <u>schottishe</u> steps <u>on in original direction</u> to greet new opposites in same fashion.
Merry, merry, merry Christmas.		Again release partner's r.h. and shake hs with opposites.
Sheep in fold, shine like gold,	B	<u>Retain</u> l.hs with partner <u>r.hs with new opposite</u> (M with W) in a squashed circular chain (W back-to-back in centre) and with M leaning out and with 2 schottische steps, <u>wheel</u> cw as close as possible to once around.
As the day is dawning.		Release l.hs, and <u>r.h. turn opposite</u> once around.
Riding by, stockmen cry		<u>Retaining opposite's r.h. resume l.h. hold with partner and wheel</u> the line-of-4 again.
'Welcome, Christmas morning.'		Again release l.hs, and <u>r.h.turn opposite</u> once around, finishing releasing opposite and resuming high promenade hold with partner facing original direction.

Golden day. When we say
Merry, merry Christmas
In the street, where we meet,
Merry, merry, merry Christmas.
And with pride, far and wide,
All our homes adorning,
Earth and sky, sound the cry,
'Welcome, Christmas morning.'

So with joy man and boy,
Sing with us together;
On this morn, Christ was born.
Merry, merry, merry Christmas.
Raise the song, loud and strong,
In the shining weather.
Joys bells ring, Christ the king,
Merry, merry, merry Christmas.

Here is another Australian carol by writer John Wheeler and composer William James. Though not as well-known as 'Carol of the Birds', and though focussing more on people than landscape, this tune is equally evocative. To match the carol's interest in the social side to Christmas, here is a dance which has couples greeting other couples and with every exclamation of 'Merry, merry Christmas' couples shake hands - first men with men women with women, then men with women and vice-versa.

The dance features in its B part a figure used in the German folk dance 'Kreuzkönig'. Though this German dance is in a triple-time ländler rhythm (waltz-like step), this dance is done with a schottische step. To get the most of the wheeling in line it is recommended that M lean out and raise their l.elbow to make a straight line with their l.forearm and partners' l.arm (their joined l.hs just below his chin) and the W lean back a little against the joined r.arms behind them. To avoid colliding with the other pair when two-hand turning opposite, pull a little away from the others, and to make sure you get completely around with just 4 steps take each other's l.elbow in your l.h.or twist vertical r.forearms around the opposites vertical r.forearm - or both.

Variant: A simple alternate figure for the B part is a 4 hand chain, 4 steps for each hand, always giving hand to person of opposite sex, r.h. to opposite, l.h. to partner, r.h. to opposite then l.h. to partner and into high promenade hold ready to travel on to new opposites.

38. O Come All Ye Faithful

Form 2 or 3 adjacent 4 to 6 couple long improper longways sets. **Start** either foot (though all starting r.f. might look better). **Prepare for** walking/march steps throughout. **Finish each** sequence with a new partner in a new position. **Play and dance** the 20-bar march sequence **6 times** for all to arrive back with original partner in original position.

O come, all ye faithful,
Joyful and triumphant,
O come ye, O come ye to
Bethlehem;

Come and behold Him,
Born the King of Angels;
O come, let us adore Him,
O come, let us adore Him,

O come, let us adore Him,
Christ, the Lord.

See how the shepherds
Summoned to his cradle,
Leaving their flocks to graze,
draw nigh in holy fear!
We, too, will thither
Bend our hearts' oblations.
- *Chorus* -

Lo, star-led chieftains,
Magi, Christ adoring,
Offer him incense,
gold and myrrh;
We to the Christ-child
Bring our hearts' oblations.
- *Chorus* -

Child, for us sinners,
Poor and in the manger,
Fain we embrace thee
with love and awe:
Who would not love thee,
Loving us so dearly?
- *Chorus* -

Sing, choirs of angels,
Sing in exultation,
O sing all ye bright
host of heaven above;
Glory to God,
All glory in the highest.
- *Chorus* -

A   Facing partner up and down contra lines go forward and, except for top couples who face down and take inside hs, back.

B   Top couples lead down between lines to bottom. As they pass, others lead up and, starting with new tops, every second couple, turns to face down set.

C   Taking hs in facing lines running across the set, go forward towards opposite and, except for couples on right (viewed from top), back.

D   Couples on right lead between lines to other side. As they pass, others lead along and, starting with the new pair on far right, every second couple, turn about to face across set.

E   Takes hs in minor sets of 2 couples and circle once around, finishing opening out into lines up and down, facing new (temporary) partner across column.

This carol is sung in dozens of languages all around the world. The original Latin text, 'Adeste Fideles', was long thought to be the work of the 13th century mystic Bonaventura, but the discovery of a mid-18th century manuscript suggests it was in fact written by John Francis Wade (1711-86), a convert to Roman Catholicism born in Leeds. Whether Wade composed the tune that accompanied the text or borrowed it from another source is not, however, clear (the tune has some similarity with one in a comic opera produced in Paris in 1744). The English version of the text given here is based on a translation of verses 1 to 3 and 6 made by the choral revivalist Frederick Oakeley (1802-80) in 1841 for the use of his London congregation. William Brook (1848-1917), a London hymn enthusiast, later supplied translations for verses 4 and 5.

This dance will have the faithful marching in every direction with constantly changing partners and neighbours. For all to arrive magically back in place after 6 verses, it is best to have 3 adjacent longways sets each with 6 couples - i.e. 36 dancers in grand square. Other size sets are possible, simply requiring less or more concentration and fewer or more verses for all to arrive back home. If danced in a small 2 column wide 8 couple set, the promenades between the lines can be quite leisurely and you end up with 4 circles. In a large 4 column wide 32 couple set the promenade may need to be a brisk face-to-face 2h galop and you end up with a challenging 8 circles at the end. In any case, whether leading down from the top or across the set from the side, the promenade is always performed with the W on the M's r.h. side - the natural side.

Yea, Lord we greet thee, / Born this happy morning, /Jesus, to thee / be all glory given; / Word of the Father, / Now in flesh appearing.
- *Chorus* -

39. The Old Year Away is Fled

Form a circle of as many couples as will holding hs. **Start** M l.f. W r.f.. **Prepare for** polka (or Scottish travelling) steps. **Finish sequence** having progressed one place, M along l.o.d.. W against. **Play** and **dance** the 16-bar jig sequence **as many times as will**.

The old year now away is fled, the new year it is entered;	A1	All <u>in</u> with 2 polka steps (or Scottish travelling steps), <u>and</u> retire <u>out</u> with 2 polka steps.
Then let us all our sins down tread, and joyfully all appear.	A2	With 4 polka steps, releasing corner, <u>M turns to partner</u> and goes cw around her, <u>wrapping her up</u> on his r.arm as she, r.h. raised, turns over l.sh., <u>then</u> joining front hs <u>in sweetheart hold,</u> they wheel cw as a couple, finishing facing along l.o.d.
Let's merry be this holiday, and let us run with sport and play,	B1	With 2 polka steps <u>M rolls W out</u> and she, again r.arm raised, turns 1½ over her r.sh. <u>till M's r.h. holds her l.h. behind her back</u>, then M's takes her r.h. in his l.h. (elbow extended) <u>and they wheel</u> cw, finishing again facing along l.o.d.
Hang sorrow, let's cast care away	B2	With 2 polka steps <u>M</u> raises and <u>goes under W's r.arm</u>, releasing her l.h. from his r.h. but retaining her r.h. in his l.h. <u>to finish</u> in exchanged positions <u>facing in.</u>
God send us a merry new year!		With 2 polka steps, <u>balance</u> on joined inside hs <u>towards</u> partner (touching free hs palm-to-palm) <u>then</u> (pushing with outside hs) <u>away</u> opening out <u>into circle</u>.

And now with new year's gifts each
friend unto each other they do send;
God grant we may our lives amend,
and that truth may now appear.
Now like the snake cast off your skin
of evil thoughts and wicked sin,
And to amend this new year begin -
God send us a merry new year!

And now let all the company
in friendly manner all agree,
For we are here welcome all may see
unto this jolly good cheer.
I thank my master and my dame,
the which are founders of the same,
To eat and drink now is no shame -
God send you a happy new year!

Come lads and lasses every one,
Jack, Tom, Dick, Bess, Mary and Joan,
Let's cut the meat unto the bone,
for welcome you need not fear.
And here for good liquor you shall not
lack, / 'twill whet my brains and
strengthen my back / This jolly good
cheer it must go to wrack -
God send us a happy new year!

The lyric offered here is from *New Christmas Carols*, 1642 where it is said to go 'to the tune of Greensleeves'. Though some ascribe authorship of the latter to Henry VIII there is no evidence for this. Greensleeves was first registered in 1580 to a Richard Jones. Shakespeare mentioned it by name twice in *The Merry Wives of Windsor* - hired bands of musicians being said to play it slowly as traitors were hanged.

With a lyric too wordy to mime, this dance simply attempts to capture the spirit of this carol. The A part opens with a rousing communal figure before the man brings his new partner into a sweet embrace. The B part opens with a merry figure in which the W twirls out of one cosy hold into another (easy if she keeps her r.h. n a plane slightly higher than their l.h.), and ends with a brief greeting and farewell as all sing 'God send us a merry new year!' The dance works best when the carol is interpreted as a lively jig - with 1 skip or 'polka' step for every bar. For a slow interpretation it would be better to switch to the dance offered under *What Child is This*, and take 2 waltz steps where here you take 1 polka step.

Come give us good liquor when I do call,
I'll drink to each one in this hall,
I hope that loud I must not bawl,
so unto me lend an ear.
Good fortune to my master send,
and to our dame which is our friend,
God bless us all, and so I end -
God send us a happy new year!

John Garden, *The Christmas Carol Dance Book*, December 2002

40. O Little Town of Bethlehem

Form circles of 5 couples holding hs. **Start** l.f.. **Prepare for** schottische/chassé steps (3 steps and lift - alternating starting foot) throughout. **Finish sequence** M having progressed one place acw, W cw around set. **Play and dance** the 16-bar schottische **5 times** for all to return to original partner in original place.

O little town of Bethlehem,
How still we see thee lie.
Above thy deep and dreamless sleep
The silent stars go by.
Yet in thy dark streets shineth
The everlasting light.
The hopes and fears of all the years
Are met in thee tonight.

A   Circle left about ¼ way cw with 2 schottische steps.
    All in with 1 schottische step and out with 1 schottische step.
    Circle left again ¼ way round with 2 schottische steps.
    All in and out again, finishing turning to face partner.

B   Chassé to left (M in W out) then right to face partner, put r.arm around other's waist and turn once cw with 2 schottische steps.

C   Chassé on own forward left diagonal (M in W out) to draw level with partner then on right diagonal behind partner, take 2hs with next, turn once cw with 2 schottische steps and open out into circle.

O morning stars, together
Proclaim the holy birth!
And praises sing to God the King,
And peace to men on earth!
For Christ is born of Mary,
And gathered all above,
While mortals sleep the angels keep
Their watch of wondering love.

This hymn by the American Episcopalian priest, reformer and humanitarian, Phillip Brooks, was inspired by a journey he had undertaken from Jerusalem to Bethlehem. Of a midnight service there on Christmas Eve 1865 he wrote:

> I remember standing in the old church in Bethlehem, close to the spot where Jesus was born, when the whole church was ringing hour after hour with splendid hymns of praise to God, how again and again it seemed as if I could hear voices I knew well, telling each other of the wonderful night of the savior's birth.

How silently, how silently
The wondrous gift is given!
So God imparts to human hearts
The blessings of his heaven.
No ear may hear his coming;
But in this world of sin,
Where meek souls will receive him still,
/ The dear Christ enters in.

The hymn was written two years later in 1867. It was included in several late-19th century American hymnals and then in the 1906 *English Hymnal* where it was noted that Brooks 'skilfully brings the reader from the contemplation of the scene itself to an awareness of its meaning for the individual believer'. Four tunes are commonly associated with the carol. The North Americans usual sing the melody of St Louis, written by Brooks' organist, Lewis Redner, to whom the tune came on Christmas Eve, and was first sung the next day or to 'Ephratah', by Uzziah C. Burnap, 1895. In Britain it is to either 'Christmas Carol' by Walford Davies, London, 1905, or to 'Forest Green' (given above) a traditional English folk tune arranged by Vaughan Williams. The dance works equally well to all.

Where children pure and happy
Pray to the blessed child,
Where misery cries out to thee,
Son of the mother mild;
Where charity stands watching
And faith holds wide the door,
The dark night wakes, the glory breaks,
And Christmas comes once more.

In the dance you trace the old wall and narrow streets of Bethlehem. Each time through the sequence, after reckoning in both circling ½ way in the A part and then going 1/10 of the way in opposite directions when performing the progression in the B part, M progress exactly 2/5 of the way cw around set, W 3/5 cw. The 5 'sides' of the circle therefore always remain intact, it is just that the occupants of the sides change. Magically, after 5 times through, you will have danced with all possible partners and finish back close to original position with original partner.

O holy child of Bethlehem,
Descend to us, we pray;
Cast out our sin and enter in,
Be born in us today.
We hear the Christmas angels
The great glad tidings tell,
O come to us, abide with us,
Out Lord Emmanuel !

John Garden, *The Christmas Carol Dance Book*, December 2002

41. Once in Royal David's City

Form 2 parallel improper columns (A and B, A is on the band's left) of an equal and even number of couples. **Start** either foot. **Prepare for** brisk walking. **Finish sequence** having progressed one place up or down ready to repeat sequence with same neighbours to side but with new opposites. **Play and dance** the 32-bar sequence **as many times as will**.

Once in Royal David's city	A1	With 6 steps all 1s and 2s circle 4 hs left once around then with 2 steps release opposites and M leads partner a little to left until 1s of column B can face off with 2s of column A.
Stood a lowly cattle shed,		With 8 steps 1s from B & 2s from A circle once left in middle, release and lead left while 2s from B & 1s from A lead out and trace a wide semi-circle around to face back in opposite direction.
Where a mother laid her baby	A2	With 6 steps 2s circle with each other in the B column while 1s circle in the A column, then with 2 steps M all lead partner to left.
In a manger for his bed.		With 8 steps 2s from B circle with 1s from A in middle release and lead left while others lead out and make a wide loop around.
Mary was that mother mild	B	All 8 dancers in adjacent minor sets take hs (pair of 1s and pair of 2s) and with 8 steps circle left ½ way to finish back in place.
Jesus Christ her little child.		With 8 steps lines-of-4 pass through by r.sh., releasing hs to turn single over r.sh. (nose-to-nose with opposite) as you pass through.

He came down from earth to heaven
Who is God and Lord of all
And his shelter was a stable
And his cradle was a stall,
With the poor and mean and lowly
Lived on earth our Saviour holy.

And through all his wondrous childhood he would honour and obey/ Love,
and watch the lowly maiden/ In whose
gentle arms he lay./ Christian children
all must be/ Mild, obedient, good as he.

For he is our childhood's pattern
Day by day like us he grew;
He was little, weak and helpless;
Tears and smiles like us he knew;
And he feeleth of our sadness,
And he shareth in our gladness.

And our eyes at last shall see him,
Through his own redeeming love;
For that Child so dear and gentle
Is our Lord in heaven above;
And he leads his children on
To the place where he is gone.

Not in that poor lowly stable,/ With the
oxen standing by,/ We shall see him, but
in heaven,/ Set at God's right hand on
high, When, like stars, his children
crowned/All in white shall wait around.

This hymn was written by Mrs C.F. Alexander. Born Cecil Frances Humphrey in Dublin in 1818, the daughter of an English army officer, she married the Tractarian clergyman William Alexander in 1850. Although her work invariably goes under her married, she wrote most of her hymns before she was married. This one was first published in 1848 in her *Hymns for Little Children*. Although some elements seem a bit precious today (and verse 3 is often dropped from modern hymn books), Ian Bradley in *The Penguin Book of Carols* notes that it goes further to recognising Jesus' humanity ('tears and smiles like us he knew') than does, for example, 'Away in the Manger' ('the little Lord Jesus, no crying he makes'). The tune to which the hymn is set was by Henry Gauntlett (said to have composed more than 10,000 hymn tunes). Gauntlett was born in Shropshire, England, in 1805, become an organist and choirmaster at a young age, practised as a solicitor, retired to devote himself to music, and published his setting for this hymn in 1849.

This dance, like that for 'O Come All Ye Faithful', plays with the possibility of dancing not just up and down a column, but across adjacent ones. If you have 4 rows with 4 dancers in each (a nice square image for an ancient city) and you dance the sequence 7 times (perhaps to all 6 verses then the first again) you will arrive back where you start. Just remember to loop wide on the ends to give the others time to complete their circle and disengage. This is a very dizzy dance, but then so was the one King David was said to have danced on the day of his coronation, when shedding most of his cloths, he whirled half naked and 'with all his might' in front of the Arc of Covenant. To recapture some of this dervish spirit, I suggest following the cw circling with a cw turn single as you pass through (though I'm not insisting you do it naked). If it is too dizzy for your taste you can dance it to a standard 64 beat walking tune and add a forward and back before and after the pass through.

John Garden, *The Christmas Carol Dance Book*, December 2002

42. On Christmas Night

Form a column of 4 couples, top 2 couples facing down, bottom 2 couples facing up, for all W on right of M. **Start** either foot. **Prepare for** brisk walking steps. **Finish sequence** with new partner in opposite role (if a middle, now an end, if an end now a middle, and facing in at right angles to previous orientation. **Play and dance** the 16-bar jig sequence **4 times** to rotate all the way back to original partner in original position.

On Christmas night all Christians sing	A1	Dance <u>waves</u> in own half of column, end couple arch in over retiring middles with 4 steps
To hear the news the angels bring.		then <u>reverse</u> roles to place with 4 steps.
On Christmas night all Christians sing	A2	<u>Repeat</u>.
To hear the news the angels bring.		
News of great joy news of great mirth,	B	With 4 steps <u>middles lead out</u> opposite away from partner *while* ends lead in, turn back on partner and take and raise opposite's inside hand.
News of our		
merciful King's birth.		With 8 steps dance outward-facing <u>waves-on-the side</u> with rear couple again making arch over retiring front couple and back (not repeated), <u>then</u>, with 4 steps flow into ½ 2h turn with person in hand and face in from new position.

Then why should men on earth be sad
Since our Redeemer made us glad?
Then why should men on earth be sad
Since our Redeemer made us glad?
When from our sin he set us free,
All for to / gain our liberty?

When sin departs before his grace
Then life and health come in its place
When sin departs before his grace
Then life and health come in its place
Angels and men with joy may sing,
All for to / see the new born King.

All out of darkness we have light
Which made the angels sing this night
All out of darkness we have light
Which made the angels sing this night
Glory to God and peace to Men,
Now and for / ever more, Amen.

Though often called 'Sussex Carol' after the region in which it was collected by Cecil Sharp and Vaughan Williams from Mrs Verrall of Monk's Gate in the early 20th century, the carol was first published in a work by an Irish bishop, Luke Wadding, *Small Garland of Pious and Godly Songs*, Ghent, 1684. It is not clear whether Wadding wrote the song or was recording an earlier composition. The tune to which it is sung today is the one Williams took down from Mrs Verrall and published in 1919.

The dance is in the same formation is as the beautiful 1651 Playford collection dance 'Lull me Beyond Thee', though the progression used here is unique to this dance. Each time through the sequence dancers will find themselves one quarter of the way around the set, in a new role (if they were a middle/front dancer they become an end/rear dancer) and with a new partner. Though the axis of the dance shifts each time through the sequence by 90 degrees, the dance always starts and finishes with couples facing in toward centre of set, woman on the man's right. After 4 verses of the carol all will arrive back in their starting position with their partner - so long as dancers have avoided all temptation to hesitate! Don't dally in the waves, don't stop to take hands with opposite before leading them out on the angle (and straight away go shoulder-to-shoulder or make an arch ready for side waves), and don't be put off by the musical phrasing in the B part, just flow through the side arches into the ½ 2h turn with a new partner.

John Garden, *The Christmas Carol Dance Book*, December 2002

43. O Tannenbaum

♩ = 130 [A]

Chords: C G C Dm | 1. G G⁷ C | 2. G⁷ C [Intro.]
C Am Dm G C G Am Dm G G⁷ C

Form a circle of as many couples as will holding hs. **Start** M l.f. W r.f.. **Prepare for** waltz, chassé, balancing, hobble mazurka and running steps. **Finish sequence** W having progressed on along l.o.d. to new partner. **Play and dance** the 16-bar waltz/mazurka sequence **as many times as will.**

O Tannenbaum, O Tannenbaum,
wie grün sind deine Blätter!
O Tannenbaum, O Tannenbaum,
wie grün sind deine Blätter!

Du grünst nicht nur zur Sommerszeit,
nein auch im Winter, wenn es schneit.

O Tannenbaum, O Tannenbaum,
wie treu sind deine Blätter!

O Tannenbaum, O Tannenbaum,
du kannst mir sehr gefallen!
O Tannenbaum, O Tannenbaum,
du kannst mir sehr gefallen!
Wie oft hat doch zur Weihnachtszeit
ein Baum von dir mich hoch erfreut
O Tannenbaum, o Tannenbaum,
du kannst mir sehr gefallen!

O Tannenbaum, o Tannenbaum,
dein Kleid soll mich was lehren:
O Tannenbaum, o Tannenbaum,
dein Kleid soll mich was lehren:
die Hoffnung und Beständigkeit
gibt Trost und Kraft zu jeder Zeit.
O Tannenbaum, o Tannenbaum,
dein Kleid will mich was lehren.

(A traditional English paraphrase)

O Christmas tree, O Christmas tree,
How steadfast are your branches!
O Christmas tree, O Christmas tree,
How steadfast are your branches!
Your boughs are green in summer's clime
And through the snows of winter time.
O Christmas tree, O Christmas tree,
How steadfast are your branches!

A1 All go in with 2 waltz steps.
Balance to face neighour and to partner.

A2 Take 2hs with neighbour and 2 slow chassé steps out of circle.
2 waltz steps to 2h turn as a couple ¾ way, finishing opening out and facing along l.o.d.

B Balance away, towards.
Travel forward as you mirror turn twice about (M acw to left W cw to right) with 2 mazurka hobble steps (step, together, hop), finishing in waist-shoulder hold

A3 2 mazurka hobble steps forward along the l.o.d..
With 6 running steps wheel ¾ (W back M forward) to finish facing in holding hs in a circle.

This carol takes us back to ancient pagan winter solstice celebrations. The practice of bringing a fir tree into the house at Christmas time and decorating seems to have begun in the Rhineland in the late Middle ages, and was then brought to Britain by the German Prince Albert. The words are a Christianised version of an old German folk-song made by Ernst Anschütz, a Leipzig schoolmaster, in 1824, and the tune to which Anschütz set the words was that of a popular song of his day, which was in turn a borrowing from a traditional students' song. The words have since had many different English translations/versions (many, unfortunately, overly archaic, rhythmically awkward or poetically forced) and the tunes used in many other contexts - including very political ones.

In this dance, to match the provenance of the carol, I have sequenced some typical German waltz and mazurka steps. Using these steps dancers in the A part trace the shape of a Christmas tree and in the B part mime the stringing of the decorative tinsel and spinning of the baubles and stars.

44. Past Three O'Clock

Form scattered circles of 3 people, no partner necessary. **Start** l.f.. **Prepare for** brisk travelling waltz steps (or running steps in triple time). **Finish sequence** with a new leader ready to start the knot. **Play and dance** the 16-bar bourrée sequence as many times as will.

Past three o'clock,
On a cold frosty morning.
Past three o'clock:
Good morrow, masters all!
Born is a Baby / Gentle as may be,
Son of th' eternal / Father supernal

A   Lead dancer brings joined hs onto r.hip, pulls back l.sh. to turn out of set away from others, bends down, turns cw about under own hs, rises, pulls on r.h. then l.h. to unravel back into a circle.

B   Circle left with 8 bourrée steps, finishing with new member of trio ready to lead (Option explained below of mixing sets every turn or ever 3 turns).

- Chorus -
Seraph quire singeth,
Angel bell ringeth,
Hark how they rime it,
Time it and chime it!

The refrain and the tune go back to Renaissance times and both were possibly traditional ones used by the waits. Both are found in 17th century sources. The words of the refrain were used, for example, in the 1665 edition of John Playford's *Dancing Master*, the 3rd edition, and were quoted or used in literature and song many times in the 18th and 19th centuries. A volume of *Old English Ditties* published in 1881 included a non-Christmas song with this refrain complemented by verses composed by John Oxenford. The Christmas verses given here and now most commonly associated with the refrain and the melody were written by George Ratcliff Woodward, who also wrote the words to 'Ding, Dong, Merrily on High', for *The Cambridge Carol Book* of 1924, which he co-edited.

- Chorus -
Mid earth rejoices
Hearing such voices
Ne'ertofore so well
Carolling 'Nowell'

- Chorus -
Hinds o'er the pearly
Dewy lawn early
Seek the high stranger
Laid in the manger.

The A part of this dance, the part to which you return to finish the dance as well, features a 3-person Austrian ländler figure.

- Chorus -
Cheese from the dairy
Bring they for Mary,
And, not for money,
Butter and honey.

Variants: There are many other knot figures which can also be used in this same space of time as the one give here, so dancers should feel free to vary the figure if they wish. One variant changes one member of the circle at the end of the turn and might be done either every time or every 3rd time. To do this, instead of simply circling on the B part, the person who led the knot releases l.h. and following outstretched l.h. leads their line-of-3 off to join with new line of 3 in circle of 6, then releases r.h. so that former middle person in each line leads next 3 into a new circle of 3. If a line-of-3 does not manage to find another line in time to swap leaders, they can simply circle up in same line-of-3 and take a new leader among their own. In either case, as the last note in verse is held new leader prepares to execute the knot in their circle of 3.

- Chorus -
Light out of star-land
Leadeth from far land
Princess to meet him,
Worship and greet him.

- Chorus -
Myrrh from full coffer
Incense they offer;
Nor is the golden
Nugget witholden.

- Chorus -
Thus they: I pray you,
Up, sirs, nor stay you
Till ye confess him
Likewise, and bless him.
- Chorus -

45. Patapatapan

Form a circle of as many couples as will, M facing along l.o.d. holding r.h. with W facing against the l.o.d.. **Start** l.f..
Prepare for doubles and singles. **Finish sequence** having progressed one place along, M acw (along l.o.d.) W cw (against l.o.d.). **Play and dance** the 13-bar 'gavotte' sequence **as many times as will**. N.B. Lyric starts just before the strain mark, dance pattern with the strain mark. N.B.B. Can also be danced in longways set snowballing from the top.

Willie, take your little drum,

Robin, bring your fife, and come,
And be merry while you play.
Turelurelu. Patapatapan.
Come be merry while you play,
On this joyous Christmas day.

God and man became today,
More in tune than fife and drum,
So be merry while you play.
- Chorus -
Come be merry while you play,
On this joyous Christmas day.

When the men of olden days,
Gave the King of Kings their praise
They had pipes on which to play
- Chorus -
They had drums on which to play
Full of joy on Christmas day.

A L.f. double to <u>r.h. turn partner ½ way to</u> take l.hs with neighbours and <u>form waves</u>, M facing out, W in.
  All <u>balance right and left</u>.
  With <u>r.f. double twirl over r.sh.</u> across <u>to other side of partner</u>.
B L.f. single to 'balance' <u>left</u>, r.f. single to '<u>balance' right</u>.
C L.f. double to <u>l.h. turn</u> partner <u>½ way</u> into progressed position.
  <u>Both step onto r.f as M</u> takes r.hs with new W and kisses the taken hand while he bows and she curtsies.

This carol was written by the famous Burgundian Bernard de la Monnoye (1641-1728) using one of the dialects which once flourished in Central France. The tune was either traditional or written by Monnoye himself. Guillo and Robin were stock characters signifying 'the whole village', the 'tamborin' a small elongated drum hung from the shoulders and the 'fleute' either the 3-hole pipe (as in pipe and tabor) or the fife (as in fife and drum). 'Turelurelu' is the sound of the latter and 'patapatapan' of the former. The original Burgundian lyrc was:

> Guillô, pran ton tamborin, / Toi, pran tu fleute, Robin. /
> Au son de cés instruman. / *- Chorus -*
> Au son de cés instruman. / Je diron Noei gaiman.

In the first half of the dance dancers give r.hs to 'take your little drum', give the other hand into a wave for 'bring your fife…', and twirl happily to 'be merry while you play'. The second part of the dance plays more on tune's gavotte-like nature and traditionally in a gavotte the men took it in turn to kiss all the women. Inspired by this notion, in the second half of this sequence I have choreographed in a progression and a kiss. Men don't take turns kissing all the women at one go, but will nevertheless eventually all get to kiss all the women. Indeed, the moment when all return to their partner (M kissing her r.h.) may be a good moment to stop the dance. As after every other kiss you will want to dance on starting l.f., it is important that after stepping onto your r.f. to take hs with a new partner, that you keep your weight on this r.f. while greeting.

Variant: Form a longways proper set and start with just the top couple. They finish in exchanged places face down and dance with their respective 2nd couple opposite. Continue thus (M progressing cw around set, W acw) till all are dancing and taking hs when possible with neighbours. When leaders reach the bottom they dance again with their partner but after the l.h. turn, they retain l.hs, throw the r.h. over the top into a skater's hold facing up on original side. They wait as the couple behind them, finding they can progress no further around the circle, do the same (give r.h. across to their partner, do the figure across the set, and finish on original side). When all have formed a column in inverted order, follow the new top couple as they caste as a couple out to the left - top couple going to bottom, bottom couple coming up to top. All wheel into original positions, face partners then push back into a bow.

John Garden, *The Christmas Carol Dance Book*, December 2002

46. Personent Hodie

Form a circle of as many as will, no partner needed, all holding hs. **Start** l.f.. **Prepare for** doubles, singles and grapevine steps. **Finish sequence** all with same neighbours but having moved a little acw around the circle. **Play and dance** the 18-bar sequence **as many times as will**.

On this day earth shall ring
with the song children sing
to the Lord, Christ our King,
born on earth to save us,
Him the father gave us,
Id-e-o-o-o,
id-e-o-o-o,
ideo, gloria
in excelsis Deo!

His the doom, ours the mirth;
when he came down to earth,
Bethlehem saw his birth;
ox and ass beside him
from the cold would hide him.
- *Chorus* -

God's bright star, o'er his head,
Wise men three to him led;
kneel they low by his bed,
lay their gifts before him,
praise him and adore him.
- *Chorus* -

On this day angels sing;
with their song earth shall ring,
praising Christ, heaven's King,
born on earth to save us;
peace and love he gave us.
- *Chorus* -

A Double left (step left, bring r.f. up, onto l.f. again, and pause).
  Double <u>right</u> (step right, left together, right, pause).
  Double <u>left</u>.
  Double <u>right</u>.
  <u>Single left, single right</u>.
B <u>Step onto left, kick left and right</u>.
  <u>Step onto right, kick right and left</u> .
  <u>Single left, single right</u>.
  <u>Grapevine</u> with 4 steps, stepping to side with left, behind with right, left to side, and right in front.

This happy 15th or 16th century Latin carol is probably a parody of an earlier medieval song beginning 'intonent hodie voces ecclesie' in honour of St Nicholas, the patron saint of Russia, sailors and children (to whom he traditionally brings gifts on his feast day, 6 December). The parody may have been written for Holy Innocents' Day, a day when choristers and their boy bishop ruled the choir and displaced the senior clergy from their stalls. The tune which accompanied it in the 1582 Finnish *Piae Cantiones* manuscript was possibly that of the earlier song as a very similar melody is found in a 1360 manuscript from Moosburg, Germany. The English translation used today is by James M. Joseph.

To match this carol is a renaissance-style branle, together with a kicking passage so typical of those branle in Arbeau's 1589 *Orchesographie*. Remember 'branle' meant to sway, so try to have everyone in your line swaying in unison as you dance, and remember that you most easily kick the foot that you have weight on so it is after stepping onto the l.f. with a single left that you need to kick the l.f. and after your single right that you kick your r.f.. As for hand hold, you might try the combination depicted below - right palm down, left palm up.

John Garden, *The Christmas Carol Dance Book*, December 2002

47. Quem Pastores Laudevere

Form a double circle of as many couples as will in high promenade hold (M on inside, W on outside) facing along l.o.d.. **Start** l.f.. **Prepare for** gentle walking and chassés. **Finish sequence** having progressed on to new partner, M along l.o.d., W against. **Play and dance** the 8-bar 6/4 sequence **as many times as will**.

Quem pastores laudavere,	A	<u>Walk forward with 2 slow step</u> (l.f. then r.f.) <u>Chassé left</u> (with l, r, l, pause) <u>while about facing</u> (M remaining on inside).
Quibus angeli		<u>Travel backwards</u> along the l.o.d. <u>with 2 slow steps</u> (step onto r.f. pointing l.toe, then onto l.f. pointing r.toe).
dixere,		<u>Turn</u> about over l.sh. <u>to again face along l.o.d. with a slow</u> backwards <u>chassé starting on r.f.</u>.
'Absit vobis jam timere,	B	Take <u>2 slow steps forward, then</u> *while* M chassés in place, <u>W chassés left</u> all the way across in front of M <u>to change side</u>.
Natus est rex gloriae'		<u>W chassés back</u> to right *while* M steps in place <u>then</u> M (releasing first his l.h. then his r.h.) lets W <u>cast over their r.sh. to</u> be collected in high promenade hold by <u>a new</u> oncoming <u>M</u>.

Ad quem reges ambulabant,
Aurum, thus, myrrham portabant,
Immolabant haec sincere
Nato regi gloriae.

Exultemus cum Maria
I coelesti hierarchia,
Natum promat voce pia
Dulci cum melodia.

Christo regi Deo nato,
Per Mariam nobis dato,
Merito resonet vere
Laus, honor et gloria.

Some of the many English versions of this carol include J.M. Neale's hymn, 'Jesus, kind above all others' (itself a translation of a Latin hymn 'Jesus noster, Jesus bonus'), George Bradford Carid (1917-84) 'Shepherds came, their praises bringing…', C.S.Phillips' 'Thou whom shepherds worshipped…', James Quinn's 'Angel voices, richly blending…', J.O'Connor's 'Shepherds tell your beauteus story…' and Imogen Holst's 'Shepherd left their flocks astraying…'. The tune, together with Latin words to 3 of the 4 verses sung today and given here, were first found in a manuscript dated 1410 in the Hohenfurth Abbey in Germany. It was reproduced in several mid-16th century German song books (including Valentin Triller's *Ein schlesich Singbüchlein aus göttlicher Schrift*, Breslau, 1555). The lyric is effectively one long sentence with the main verb in the second last line. Ian Bradley's translation in *The Penguin Book of Carols*, 1999 of verses 1, 2 and 4 is:

1. To him whom the shepherd praised, being told by the angels: 'Now let fear be banished from you: the King of Glory is born'
2. To him to whom the wise men journeyed, carrying gold, frankincense and myrrh and offered these things sincerely to the victorious Lion
3. To Christ the King, born of God, given to us through Mary, let resound right worthily 'Praise, honour and glory'.

Verse 3 was later slipped in and breaks the sentence with an appeal to, 'Rejoice with Mary and the heavenly hierarchy (of angels) as they praise the infant in reverent tones and with sweet melody'.

I have written a stately dance to go with the carol, dovetailing not so much with the carol's lyric as with its curiously phrased melody - there being some phrases which lend themselves to slow single steps and others to chassés (and in this respect the pattern in the second half is slightly different to that of the first half).

48. Rejoice and Be Merry

Form a double circle of as many couples as will, M on inside facing W on outside. **Start** l.f.. **Prepare for** clapping, stomping, and waltz steps. **Finish sequence** with W having progressed along l.o.d. to new partner. **Play and dance** the 16-bar mazurka sequence **as many times as will**.

Rejoice and be merry in
song and in mirth;
O praise our Redeemer,
All mortals on earth!
For this is the birthday of
Jesus our King,
Who brought us salvation:
His praises we'll sing.

A heavenly vision
Appeared in the sky;
Vast numbers of angels
The shepherds did spy,
Proclaiming the birthday of
Jesus our King,
- Chorus -

Likewise a bright star
In the sky did appear,
Which led the wise men
From the East to draw near;
They found the Messiah,
Sweet Jesus our King,
- Chorus -

And when they were come,
they their treasures unfold,
And unto him offered
Myrrh, incense and gold.
So blessed for ever
Be Jesus our King,
- Chorus -

A   Clap own knees, sh.s, hs, then with opposite's r.hs, l.hs, both.
     Again knees, shs and hs, then take (with a clap) r.hs with opposite.
     With 3 waltz steps turn opp. r.h. 1¼ into wave M facing out again
     then stomp while taking (with a clap) l.hs with neigh.

B   With 3 waltz steps turn neighbour l.h. once around then stomp while
     taking (with a clap) r.hs over the top of l.hs.
     In cross hand hold, both starting l.f. take 4 waltz steps to turn as a
     couple, finish M on inside W outside.

This carol is also sometimes called 'The Gallery Carol' because it belongs to the tradition associated with the choirs and bands sited in the west galleries of churches before the advent of organs in the mid-19th century (see entry under 'Hail Happy Morn'). This particular carol was discovered in the early 20th century in an old Dorset west-gallery songbook and included in the *English Carol Book* of 1919. The original songbook has been lost but the original carol probably dates back to the early or mid-18th century.

To fit the jolly mazurka-like rhythm of this carol here is a dance you can do without needing to know any mazurka steps. It is composed simply of clapping, stomping and waltzing, but you can put more style into the clapping by swaying back as you clap your own knees, (then crossing own arms) shoulders and hands and then swaying forward as you clap the opposite's hands - just as German folkloric dancers do when miming hammer-swinging blacksmiths in the dance 'Die Hammerschmiedts-gselln'. Some singers like to repeat the chorus, and if that is planned, simply repeat the B part of the dance each time, before returning to the beginning of the sequence. In either case, try, whenever directed to take hands with someone to do so with a synchronised clapping of palms together. The final 4 waltz step turning-as-a-couple can be on the spot, but if all are experienced dancers the dance leader might consider recommending everyone travel along the l.o.d. as they turn.

John Garden, *The Christmas Carol Dance Book*, December 2002

49. Remember O Thou Man

Form a circle of as many couples as will, M facing acw holding 2hs with W facing cw. **Start** weight on l.f., pointing r.f.. **Prepare for** galliard steps. **Finish sequence** having progressed one place along, M cw W acw (i.e. against the direction they are originally facing). **Play and dance** the 16-bar galliard sequence **as many times as will**.

Remember, O thou man,	A	M take 1 galliard step (kick r, l, r, l spring in the air, switch to pointing r.f. as you land on r.f.) in place directly towards partner;
O thou man, O thou man		W does the same
Remember O thou man,	A2	Repeat starting on other foot (M then W)
Thy time is spent		
Remember O thou man,	B	M take 1 galliard step on original foot to turn about ½ acw over l.sh. clapping own hs upon the switch of feet, landing back to partner weight on l.f., pointing r.f.;
How thou art dead and gone,		W same as M above, finishing facing new partner.
And I did what I can:	C	Take 2hs with 1 galliard step and turn new partner ½ way cw to finish in progressed position on original foot.
Therefore repent!		Flourishing bow to one just turned, who will be new partner.

Remember Adam's fall,
O thou man, O thou man!
Remember Adam's fall
From heaven to hell!
O remember Adam's fall,
How we were condemned all
Into hell perpetual,
Therefor to dwell.

Remember God's goodness,
And promise made! *repeat*
Remember God's goodness,
How he sent his sonne, doubtlesse,
Our sinnes for to redresse,
Be not afraid.

The angels all did sing,
Upon the shepheards' hill; *repeat*
The angels all did singe,
Praises to our glorious King,
And peace to man living,
With a good will!'

Oh, the shepheards startled were,
To heare the angels sing, *repeat*
The shepheards amazed was
How it should come to passe
That Christ our Messias
Should be our King!

This carol is of 16th century origin. The text given here comes from the 'Country Pastimes' section of Ravenscroft 1611 *Melismata,* and is there headed 'A Christmas Caroll'. It was still being sung more than 250 years later, Thomas Hardy referring to it as the 'ancient and time-worn hymn' in his 1872 *Under the Greenwood Tree.*

The carol is matched with one of the most popular renaissance show-off dances - the galliard. Though usually a dance for solo man display, the exhausting footwork has been here choreographed into a sequence which is both social - with M and W sharing looks, kisses and kicks then progressing on to new partners - and physically sparing - with lots of restful bows built in.

To Bethlem did they goe, / The shepheards three; *repeat*
To Bethlem did they goe, / To see whether it were so or no,
Whether Christ were borne or no /To set man free.

As the angels before did say, / So it came to passe; *repeat*
As the angels before did say, / They found a Babe, whereas it lay
In a manger, wrapt in hay, /So poore he was.

In Bethlem he was borne, / For mankind's sake; *repeat*
In Bethlem he was borne, / For us that were forlorne,
And therefore tooke no scorne / Our flesh to take.

Give thanks to God always, / With heart most joyfully *repeat*
Give thanks to God always, / For this, our happy day:
Let all men sing and say: / 'Holy, holy!'

50. Rise up Shepherd and Follow

Form a double circle of as many couples as will facing along the l.o.d., M on inside on his r.knee holding inside hs with W on outside, M holding W's l.h. with his r.h.. **Start** with outside foot. **Prepare** for schottische steps and slow walking steps. **Finish sequence** having travelled around the l.o.d.. and progressed one place, M against l.o.d, W along l.o.d. **Play and dance** the 24-bar schottische sequence **as many times as will**.

There's a star in the East on Christmas morn, Rise up shepherd and follow.	**A1** M lowers to r.knee *while* W, with 2 schottische steps <u>dances acw around M then</u> he rises and they <u>both take 4 slow steps forward</u> (M's first movement is onto the l.f. he already has weight on).
It will lead to the place where the Saviour's born, Rise up shepherd and follow.	**A2** W on her l.knee while <u>M dances cw around W</u> with 2 schottische steps <u>then</u> she rises and they <u>both take 4 slow steps forward</u> (W's first movement is onto l.f. she already has weight on).
Leave your sheep and leave your lambs *Rise up shepherd and follow.*	**B1** <u>Schottische away</u> from partner until inside arms are outstretched, pull on joined inside hs just before releasing to schottische <u>towards partner then</u> into a short arm 'basket' hold and <u>turn as a couple</u>.
Leave your ewes and leave your rams. *Rise up shepherd and follow.*	**B2** <u>Schottische away</u> from partner, clapping on 'hop/lift' and back, but this time M goes back <u>behind partner</u> turning over r.sh. to face new on coming W, <u>then take new partner</u> in ballroom hold <u>and turn as a couple</u> 1½ cw finishing M facing along l.o.d. W against.
Follow, follow, *Rise up shepherd and follow.* *Follow the star of Bethlehem.* *Rise up shepherd and follow.*	**C** With M backing W, <u>chassé into centre</u> on M's l.diagonal looking <u>over joined hs</u>, <u>out</u> on M's r.diagonal looking <u>over shoulders</u>, <u>then turn as a couple</u>. <u>M</u> pushes on W's back with his r.h. at same time as raising his l.arm, and <u>guides W</u> acw <u>around</u> in front of <u>him</u>, then behind him, she trailing her l.arm across his stomach as she goes and he slipping r.h. under W's l.arm so as to resume ballroom hold <u>then turn as a couple</u>.

If you take good heed
to the angel's words.
Rise up shepherd and follow.
You'll forget your flocks;
you'll forget your herds.
Rise up shepherd and follow.
- Chorus -

This is a traditional American carol, first published as 'A Christmas Plantation Song' in Slave Songs of the United States, ed. W.F. Allen et.al. 1867. The songs in this collection were mostly collected during the Civil War from slaves on islands off Georgia and South Carolina. *The Shorter New Oxford Book of Carols* sees the tune as related to several British folk songs and indeed to a Welsh Christmas carol.

The dance figures echo the lyric. The reference to the 'star in the East' and to 'leading to a place' are matched with the M and W tracing circles around the other. The exaltation to follow is matched with the rising from bended knee and being led by the other. Both drift away from each other when urged to 'leave your sheep and lambs', and drift so far away when urged to 'leave ewes and rams' that they find new partners. The M mirrors the W on parallel chassés when urged to 'follow, follow', and the W traces a final orbit around the M when they are urged to 'follow the star'.

51. Riu, riu, chiu

Form a circle of as-many-couples-as-will. **Start** l.f.. Prepare for doubles and plain steps. **Finish sequence** progressed 1 place around circle (M along l.o.d W against). **Dance** 1 double or *chassé* every 2 bars. **Play** tune **as many times as will**, the pening A bein sung/played/danced only once. The variant A' that follows, with its extra counts, henceforth become the only A that is returned to.

A (4 bars x 3)   D l&r sideways *while* facing into circle / all in and out of centre with a D f. & b. ending swivelling to face partner / all D l&r sideways while facing ptner

A+ (The A strain with extra beats: 5 bars / 5 bars / 4 bars) All turn partner cw in r. back-allemande hold (plus 2 steps to relinquish hold and turn about into l.back-allemande hold / all acw turn partner (plus 2 steps to relinquish hold and face) / all D l&r sideways while facing partner (as before—or * if singers want to insert 2 extra counts into the 2nd and 4th bar of my Ac, then after your double left turn acw over your left shoulder with two steps and after your double right turn cw over your right shoulder with two steps).

B (4 bars x 2)   Zig-zag past partner with D l. on forward l. diagonal and / D r. on forward r. diagonal (to end back-to-back with former partner facing new), and then w. 2D full turn hand turn the one met opening out at the end to take hands in new circle woman on right of man.

B var. (4 bars x 2) D l&r sideways *while* facing into circle / all a D f. & b. ending swivelling to face partner.
A then A+BB x n then finish with A+

This hymn first appeared in the same anonymous Spanish music as 'Verbum caro'. The volume was entitled *Villancicos de diuersos Autores,* [...], was printed in Venice in 1556, and the only surviving copy is in Sweden, thus the common name for the work, *Cancioneiro de Uppsala*. This hymn is said in the work's contents to be no. 41 and often reported to be no. 46, but is actually on page 42v-43r. It appears in the same section of *Villancicos de Navidad* ('Carols for Christmas') as does 'Verbum caro'. I'm indebted to Charis Messalina Helena de Valence for introducing me to this carol and to *I Progetti*, the chamber choir she directs, for singing this for dance at our Christmas carol balls.

If you look (very) closely at the appended facsimile of the original score you will notice on the stave the occasion single or pair of dots. These represent places/beats to pause (and breath). Researchers and choirs have suggested and tried many different ways of setting this lyric to the tune and bringing it alive. Most involve introducing a 2/4 'breathing' pause between the three four 4/4 bar phrase in the A strain, and then in addition to these pause adding an extra bar to enable the canonisation of some lyrics before the second and third four 4/4 bar phrase in in the A variant strain. I have favoured doing without any pauses in the opening A strain, it becoming 4 bars / 4 bars / 4 bars, but admitting two pairs of breathing beats (even though at some points only one is marked) in the A variant strain so it becomes 5 bars / 5 bars / 4 bars. This is the pattern to which I have fitted my choreography, filling the first of each of those five bar passages with two steps to about face which, if dancers need a help remembering, you could make stomps. If you want to remove that 'extra' bar as well and just have a consistent 4 bar phrasing throughout the whole carol and dance, then you simply remove those two stomps from the choreography. If you want to interpret the score as needing an extra two counts inserted into my the 2nd and then again 4th bar of my Ac, then after you take the double to the left turn acw over your left shoulder with two steps and after you take the double back to the right turn cw over your right shoulder with two steps.

Spanish	English translation
The chorus:	
Riu, riu, chiu, la guarda rivera	[With a cry of] Riu, riu, chiu' the kingfisher
Dios guardó el lobo de nuestra cordera	God keeps the wolf from our lamb
El lobo rabioso la quiso morder,	The rabid wolf tried to bite her,
Mas Dios poderoso la supo defender;	But God Almighty knew how to defend her;
Quisola hazer que no pudiese pecar,	He wished to create her impervious to sin,
Ni aun original esta Virgen no tuviera.	Nor was this maid to embody original sin.
Este qu'es nacido es el gran monarca,	The newborn child is the mightiest monarch,
Cristo patriarca, de carne vestido;	Christ, our Holy Father, in flesh embodied;
Hanos redimido con se hacer chiquito,	He made himself small and so redeemed us,
Aunqu'era infinito, finito se hiciera.	He who was infinite became finite.
Muchas profecias lo han profetizado,	Many prophecies told of his coming,
Ya un nuestros dias lo hemos alcançado,	And now in our days we have seen them fulfilled.
A dios humanado vemos en el suelo,	God became man, on earth we behold him,
Y al hombre el cielo porquel lo quisiera.	And see man in heaven because he willed it so.
Yo vi mil garçones que andaban cantando,	A thousand singing angels I saw passing,
Por aquí volando, haciendo mil sones,	Flying overhead, sounding a thousand voices,
Diciendo a gascones: "Gloria sea en el cielo	Exulting, "Glory be in the heavens,
Y paz en el suelo", pues de sus naciera.	And peace on Earth, for Jesus has been born."
Este viene a dar a los muertos vida	He comes to give life to the dead,
Y viene a reparar de todos caída;	He comes to redeem the fall of man;
Es la luz del día aqueste mozuelo;	This child is the light of day,
Este es el cordero que San Juan dixera.	He is the very lamb Saint John prophesied
Mira bien que os cuadre que ansina lo oiera	This tale is true, as we will hear it,
Que Dios no pudiera hacer la más que madre.	God could not create a mother of greater spirit.
Él que era su padre hoy d'ella nació;	He who was her father, was born of her today;
Y el que la crió su hijo de dixera.	He created her, though he will say he is her son.
Pues que ya tenemos lo que deseamos,	Now we have received what we were all desiring,
Todos juntos vamos, presentes llevemos;	Let us go together to bear him gifts:
Todos le daremos muestra voluntad,	Let each give his will to the God who was willing
Pues a se igualar con el hombre viniera.	To come down to Earth to be man's equal.

John Garden, *The Christmas Carol Dance Book*, December 2002

52. Rocking Carol

Form a circle of as many couples as will, M facing along l.o.d. holding r.h. in r.h. with W facing against l.o.d.. **Start** M l.f. W r.f.. **Prepare for** chassés and walking steps. **Finish sequence** all a little further along the l.o.d., M having progressed along l.o.d., W against l.o.d.. **Play and dance** the 13-bar schottische-like sequence **as many times as will**.

Little Jesus, sweetly sleep, do not stir;	A	With **3** schottische/chassé steps <u>M backs W on</u> M's l.diagonal, <u>then</u> r.diagonal, <u>then</u> l.diagonal.
We will lend a coat of fur	B1	With 2 schottische steps <u>M turns W acw over her l.sh. 1½</u>, lowering his r.h. <u>to catch her in a backhold</u>, both side-by-side <u>facing along l.o.d</u>, her l.sh. next to his r.sh., his r.h. behind her back holding her r.h. on her r.hip, outside hs free.
We will rock you, rock you, rock you,	C1	With r.f. chassé to the right (M behind W), <u>opening out</u> so M is now on outside, his r.h. stretching <u>to</u> hold the l.h. of the W on the inside and looking at each other from <u>exchanged places</u>, <u>then swap back</u> into back hold.
We will rock you, rock you, rock you.	C2	<u>Repeat</u> above, <u>though as W swaps back</u> into armlock on M's r.side M takes her l.h. in his l.h. to finish in a cosy side-by-side promenade hold.
See the fur to keep you warm,	D	With 2 schottische steps <u>wheel</u> acw (<u>M back W forward</u>) once around.
Snugly 'round your tiny form.	B2	<u>Releasing r.hs turn l.h. ½ way</u> acw with 1 schottische step (M starting r.f. moves to the right while guiding W starting l.f. in an acw arc to the left) <u>then, releasing l.hs walk on with two steps</u> in original direction (M l, r along l.o.d., W r, l against l.o.d.) <u>reaching out with r.h. to new opposite</u>.

Mary's little baby, sleep, sweetly sleep,
Sleep in comfort, slumber deep.
We will rock you, rock you, rock you,
We will rock you, rock you, rock you.
We will serve you all we can,
Darling, darling little man.

This carol is of Czech origin. It was collected in the early 1920 by a Miss Jacubickova as 'Hajej, nynjej' and translated (very loosely) by Percy Dearmer, for *The Oxford Book of Carols* in 1928. Dearmer was a clergyman and socialist with a keen interest in contemporary concerns, social gospel and rescuing neglected English carols and introducing European carols. The final line of Dearmers's version has not appealed to everyone, and some have sought to change it, e.g. to 'Son of God and Son of Man.' The tune for the carol has a close resemblance to that of another traditional lullaby, 'Twinkle, twinkle, little star', and it is possible that this carol originally accompanied cradle rocking, a custom which began in German churches in medieval times and spread from there across Europe. The carol was popularised in the English speaking world by a recording made in the 1960s by Julie Andrews.

I have used the 'window' hold and shadowing of partner used in some Czech dances. The uneven number of bars presents a challenge - but adversity is turned to advantage as it enables the dances to start the sequence on the natural foot (M's l.f. W's r.f.) and the backhold switching figure (to the 'We will rock you' refrain) on the other foot (M's r.f., W's l.f.). The final two step advance to greet a new partner offers an opportunity to change back to the natural lead foot. If the circle is tight the first of the two steps might be forward to take hs with new partner and the second back to prepare to dance with them.

John Garden, *The Christmas Carol Dance Book*, December 2002

53. Rudolph the Red-Nosed Reindeer

Form pairs of couples facing forward along l.o.d., 2s behind 1s, M on inside W outside, holding inside hs with partner and outside hs with same gender neighbour (in front or behind) to form team. **Start** outside foot (M's l.f. W's r.f.). **Prepare for** combinations of 2 schottische steps (step, together, step, hop) and 4 step-hops throughout. **Finish sequence** in original formation, but having travelled along the l.o.d. **Play and dance** the 32-bar schottische sequence **once** through **then either stop and bring in new dancers or repeat without stopping**.

Rudolph the Red-Nosed Reindeer
Had a very shiny nose,
And if you ever saw it,
You could even say it glows.
All of the other reindeer
Used to laugh and call him names;
They never let poor Rudolph
Join in any reindeer games.
Then one foggy Christmas Eve,
Santa came to say:

'Rudolph with your nose so bright,
Won't you guide my sleigh tonight?'
Then how the reindeer loved him
As they shouted out with glee,

Rudolph the Red-Nosed Reindeer,
You'll go down in history.'

A1	Take 2 <u>schottische</u> steps <u>forward</u>.
	Take 4 <u>step-hops</u>-<u>forward</u>.
	<u>Schottische forward</u> then all let go of hs.
	With step-hops <u>solo mirror turn single</u> and retake hs.
A2	Schottische <u>forward</u> then without letting go of hs.
	With step-hops <u>rear couple arch over</u> front couple and untwist.
	Schottische <u>forward</u>.
	With step hops <u>new rear couple arch back</u> to place.
B	Schottische <u>forward</u>.
	With step-hops and releasing with front couple only releasing partner's hand <u>mirror hand cast</u> on sides to exchange places.
	Rejoin hs in harness and schottische <u>forward</u>.
	Front couple only releasing partner's h. <u>cast</u> on sides <u>to change back</u>
A3	Rejoin hs in harness and schottische <u>forward</u>.
	With step-hops and releasing hs with partner but retaining them on the side mirror <u>hand cast</u> on side once <u>all way around</u>.
	Take waist-shoulder hold with partner and schottische <u>forward</u>.
	With 4 step-hops <u>turn as a couple</u> cw once round, finish sliding into holding inside hand.

Rudolph The Red Nosed Reindeer
Johnny Marks
Reproduced by Permission of Warner/Chappell Music Australia Pty.Ltd.
Unauthorised Reproduction is Ilegal.

Johnny Marks created the character of shiny-nosed Rudolph for a publicity pamphlet as part of the Christmas sales campaign of an American mail-order company. He later turned the image into a song which cowboy star Gene Autry sung at Madison Square Garden in New York in 1949. The song went on to be one of the most successful songs of all time - with 140 million recordings by 500 different performers.

To get Rudolph all harnessed up and ready to fly down out of the Artic I've sequenced in this dance some wonderful jenkka/sottiis figures from the 4-horse carriage dance common to Finland and Sweden. You can flow without stopping from one time through the dance into a second and third time - either in same foursome, or, by switching direction with outside hand upon a prearranged prompt and harnessing yourself with a new couple in front or behind, danced in alternating roles.

Variant: You can start with just one (or a few) pairs of couples dancing, and then, by stopping after each time through the song and finding a new couples to join you and your partner, you can snowball into everyone dancing.

John Garden, *The Christmas Carol Dance Book*, December 2002

54. Sans Day Carol

Form a circle of couples in ballroom hold facing along the l.o.d.. **Start** with outside foot. **Prepare for** mazurka hobble steps or step-draw steps, and waltz steps. **Finish the sequence** having travelled as a couple around the l.o.d. **Play and dance** the 22-bar mazurka sequence **as many times as will**.

Now the holly bears a berry as	A1	With 2 hobble mazurka steps (step, together, hop) or slide with 2 step-draw togethers along l.o.d..
white as the milk,		Turn acw ½ way as a couple and both point with the toe of new outside foot.
And Mary bore Jesus who was wrapped up in silk:	A2	Repeat above, travelling over shoulder along l.o.d. then turn cw ½ way and point first foot (M's l.f., W's r.f.).
And Mary bore Jesus Christ our Saviour for to be	B	Turn ½ way acw as a couple and point second foot. Turn back cw and point first foot.
And the first tree of the greenwood it was the holly,	C1	Waltz on with 2 waltz steps. Plus a 3rd waltz step to end up looking over shoulder and point second foot along the l.o.d.
holly, holly!	D	Slide along l.o.d. then against l.o.d.
And the first tree of the greenwood,	C2	Starting with the 'unnatural foot' (the second foot - M's r.f., W's l.f.) and looking over shoulder rather than joined hs, waltz on with 2 waltz steps
it was the holly.		then take a 3rd waltz step to end up looking over hs and point first foot along the l.o.d.

Now the holly bears a berry
As green as the grass,
And Mary bore Jesus,
who died on the cross:
- *Chorus* -

Now the holly bears a berry
as black as the coal,
And Mary bore Jesus,
who died for us all:
- *Chorus* -

Now the holly bears a berry, as blood is it red,
Then trust we our Saviour, who rose from the dead:
- *Chorus* -

This carol was so named because the melody and the first 3 verses were first transcribed in the 19th century from the singing of a villager in St Day (also Sans Day, or St They - named after a Breton saint) in the parish of Gwennap, Cornwall. A 4 stanza version in Cornish was subsequently published ('Ma gron war'n gelinen') and the fourth stanza of this version was soon translated and added to the first 3.

The dance has all the character a 19th century varsovienne. Different combinations of mazurka, pointing and waltz steps were very popular across the 19th century western world - being danced in ballroom, skaters and high promenade hold from Scandinavia to Slovenia, America to Australia. The particular sequence offered here is, however, not only original, but unique in the way it requires the dancers to start the C2 part of the sequence with the M's r.f. W's l.f. and leading with the shoulder rather than the hand. This start flows naturally, however, out of the preceding figure and leads the dancers back onto their natural starting foot in natural starting position to dance the sequence again. For maximum sensation, make sure you are leaning out to share weight, almost swing, with your partner whenever you turn as a couple before each point.

John Garden, *The Christmas Carol Dance Book*, December 2002

55. Santa Claus is Coming to Town

Sheet music: ♩ = 90, key of G, 4/4 time, sections A1&2, B, A3 with chords D7, G, C, G, C, G, D7, G C G D G / G, C, G, C, A, D, A7, D / G, C, G, C, G, D7, G C D7, Am D7 G C G

Form couples facing partner and holding 2hs with partner across l.o.d. **Start** M l.f., W r.f.. **Prepare for** schottische steps throughout. **Finish sequence** with same partner further around l.o.d. **Play and dance** the 32-bar schottische **as many times as will**, perhaps swapping partners and 'snowball' the number of dancers on the floor.

You better watch out	A1	Swing outside hand and foot forward to schottische <u>face-to-face</u>.
You better not cry		Swing trailing hand and foot through to schottische <u>back-to-back</u>.
Better not pout		Join and bring trailing hand through inside to go <u>face-to-face</u>.
I'm telling you why		Bring other foot up inside and go forward in open <u>ballroom hold</u>.
Santa Claus is coming to town.		<u>Turn</u> as a couple <u>with</u> 8 <u>step-hops</u>, finishing holding hs.
He's making a list	A2	<u>W</u> schottische step on forward <u>right diagonal</u> *while* M mimes making list
And checking it twice		<u>M</u> schottische step on forward <u>left diagonal</u> *while* W mimes checking it
Gonna find out		<u>W</u> schottische on forward <u>left diagonal</u> *while* M watches her
Who's naughty and nice		<u>M</u> schottische on forward <u>right diagonal</u> *while* W prepares to be collected
Santa Claus is coming to town.		<u>Turn</u> as a couple <u>with</u> 8 <u>step-hops</u>, finishing M ready to help W spin away into outward turn
He sees you when you are sleeping	B	<u>W turns over r.sh.</u> then with partner travel forward along l.o.d
He knows when you're awake		<u>M turns over l.sh.</u> then travel with partner forward.
He knows if you've been bad or good		<u>W turn out</u> over outside sh., eye-contact <u>and (with M's hand assistance) back</u> other sh. *while* M schottische in place.
So be good for goodness sake!		<u>M turn out</u> over outside sh., eye-contact <u>and back</u> other sh. *while* W schottische in place.
O! You better watch out!	A3	<u>Repeat A1</u>
You better not cry		
Better not pout		
I'm telling you why		
Santa Claus is coming to town		

except on last 4 steps M turn W out under his raised l.h. to face and bow. *Option* to repeat whole sequence, and last time repeat 2 bars 'Santa Clause is coming' x 3 before playing 'to town' in order to take 16 step-hop off floor.

Lyricist Haven Gillespie and composer J. Fred Coots had already enjoyed considerable success together when they wrote this Christmas song in 1932. Initially no music publisher was interested in such an 'uncommercial kiddie tune'. Finally, in 1934 Coots' friend comedian Eddie Cantor, to please his wife Ida, who liked the song, sang it on his radio programme. It became a hit.

To make the most of these lyrics, try for good eye-contact as you come face-to-face on 'you'd better watch out', a full back-to-back as 'you'd better not cry' and a big smile as you come face-to-face for 'you'd better not pout'. The secret to an easy step-hop turn is the same as that for an easy pivot. You always put your r.f. between your partner's feet and your l.f. around the outside of your partner's feet - as the M starts l.f. he starts putting his foot around the outside while the W puts her r.f. between his feet. If you want to travel on the pivot then push forward along the l.o.d. with every r.f. step. You can either start with everyone dancing and repeating with same partner, or start with just one experienced couple dancing, and they take different partners for the second time through, thus spreading their experience with each repetition till all are dancing.

56. Silent Night

Form square sets of 4 couples holding hs facing in. **Start** M l.f., W r.f.. **Prepare for** travelling waltz steps throughout **Finish sequence** beside new partner with M having travelled one place (ie ¼ way) acw around set, W 2 places (ie ½ way). **Play and dance** the 24-bar sequence **four times** to arrive back in original place with original partner.

Silent night,	A	Without letting go of hs and with M assisting by raising r.h. <u>W turn in</u> over r.sh. <u>under raised l.h.</u> to face out, l.arm crossed over r.arm.
holy night!		Without letting go and M assisting <u>W turn back out</u> into circle.
All is calm,		<u>M same</u> as W, turning in over r.sh. under own raised l.h. till facing out, l.arm over r.arm, then
all is bright.		M turning back out into circle.
Round yon virgin,	B1	Without letting go of joined hs <u>W turn in</u> again then
Mother and Child.		Both raising hs W <u>turn out *while*</u> M turn in.
Holy infant so	B2	<u>Repeat</u>, M coming out as W go in,
so tender and mild,		W coming out as M go in
Sleep in heavenly peace,	C	M release partner from his r.h. and takes with his r.h. the l.h. of his neighbour to <u>2h turn her once</u> just short of once around <u>and wrap</u> her up - he looping her l.h. with his r.h. over her head while she turns over her r.sh., so both finish side by side, M on inside, W on outside, facing acw around set.
Sleep in heavenly peace.		<u>Promenade</u> acw till M in next M's place, wheel to face in, M spin W out by releasing his l.h. and pulling his r.h., <u>and finish facing in.</u>

Silent night, holy night!
Shepherds quake at the sight.
Glories stream from heaven afar
Heavenly hosts sing Alleluia,
Christ the Savior is born!
Christ the Savior is born.

Silent night, holy night!
Son of God, love's pure light.
Radiance beams from thy holy face
With dawn of redeeming grace,
Jesus, Lord, at thy birth.
Jesus, Lord, at thy birth.

Silent night, holy night
Wondrous star, lend thy light;
With the angels let us sing,
Alleluia to our King;
Christ the Savior is born,
Christ the Savior is born!

This carol was written for 2 male voices and guitar by Joseph Mohr (1792-1848) and Franz Gruber (1787-1863), priest and organist at St Nicholas' Church in Oberndorf, Austria. According to legend it was written in haste on Christmas Eve 1818 upon finding the organ broken (some say ruined by rust, others by mice). Recently, however, a manuscript has been discovered suggesting Gruber wrote the score 2-4 years after Mohr wrote the lyrics. The carol may have been lost had not a copy of it come into the hands of Josef Strasser, a folkmusic enthusiast whose family singing group's performance of the piece at a concert in Leipzig in 1832 led to it being published in a set of four 'anonymous Tyrolean songs'. Mohr and Gruber had to take recourse to the law to have their authorship recognised. In 1863 stanzas 1 & 3 were translated from German into English by John Freeman Young, and stanzas 2 and 4 were later translated anonymous. Its cosy child-centred sentiments were well received in Victorian England and the carol has gone on to become possibly the world's favourite.

To match the provenance the carol, this dance features a knotty figure from a southern German/Austrian ländler, a style of dancing that gave rise to the waltz. In the A part when it is not your turn to go in or out don't just stand still. You can help your partner by taking 1 waltz step in to slacken and raise arms for the loop or 'unloop' and then 1 waltz step out to straighten arms for a nice flower or circle. Try to get a bit of spring from one figure to the next. The dance could be done with more couples but is neatest in a square of 4 couples and in this formation in the course of the 4 verses, you will get to dance with all possible partners, M from each corner in turn, W alternating between home and opposite place.

57. Tomorrow Shall Be My Dancing Day

Form a double circle of as many couples as will, M on inside facing W on outside, each presenting l.sh. to the other.
Start l.f.. **Prepare for** bourrée steps and step-draw steps. **Finish sequence** having made a double progression, M against l.o.d., W along l.o.d. **Play and dance** the 24 bourrée sequence **as many times as will.**

Tomorrow shall be my dancing day	A1	With 2 bourrée steps go <u>toward partner</u> l.sh. leading and turn/wheel/swing oneself acw ½ to left <u>to face</u> partner belly-to-belly, <u>then</u> return by same route <u>back to</u> original <u>place</u>.
I would my true love did so chance	A2	<u>Repeat.</u>
To see the legend of my play,	B	Bourrée <u>in</u> to be belly-to-belly, <u>then</u> instead of retiring to own place <u>cross</u> to opposite's place, pulling r.sh. back and turning/twirling cw once about to present l.sh. from opposite side.
To call my true love to my dance.		Go <u>in</u> to face <u>then and cross back</u> to place.
Sing Oh my love,	C	<u>Take l.hs and greet</u> with a l.f. step near and r.f. draw up while raising joined l.hs to eye level.
Oh my love, my love, my love		<u>Step back</u> with r.f. step and l.f. draw then sink <u>into reverance</u> on bended r.knee.
This have I done for my true love	D	<u>Chain on</u> by giving r.h. to r.diagonal neighbour then l.h. to new partner, M again on inside W on outside.

Then was I born of a virgin pure,
From her I took fleshly substance.
Thus was I knit to man's nature
To call my true love to my dance. *etc*

In a manger laid and wrapped was I
So very poor it was my chance
Between an ox and a silly poor ass
To call my true love to my dance. *etc*

Then afterwards baptised I was,
The Holy Ghost on me did glance,
My Father's voice heard from above
To call my true love to my dance *etc*

Into the desert I was led,
Where I fasted without substance.
The devil bade me make stones my
bread, / To have me break my true love's
dance. *etc*

The Jews on me they made great suit,
And with me made great variance,
Because they loved darkness rather than
light, / To call my true love to my dance.
etc

For thirty pence Judas me sold,
His covetousness for to advance:
'Mark whom I kiss, the same do hold!'
The same is he shall lead the dance. *etc*

Although this carol has Jesus refer to mankind as 'his love' and to living as 'my dance' - imagery many find very modern - the carol is probably very old. It was first published in Sandys' 1833, *Christmas Carols, Ancient and Modern*, and probably goes back to medieval times. Indeed, there are many precidents for the use of inter-personal love motifs in spiritual work (see the *Song of Songs*) and the use of dance as a metaphor for living (see Sir John Davies 16th century poem, *Orchestra*). This carol has close parallels with a number of 15th century carols in which the infant foretells his future to his mother. The line 'To see the legend of my play' suggests it may have originally been part of a medieval mystery play, in the same way as was the 'Coventry Carol', but perhaps in this case (some suspect), part of one of the three-day religious plays performed in the Cornish language in the 14th and 15th century.

Before Pilate the Jews me brought, / Where Barabbas had deliverance;
They scourged me and set me at nought, / Judged me to die to lead the dance. *etc*

Then on the cross hanged I was, / Where a spear my heart did glance;
There issued forth both water and blood, / To call my true love to my dance. *etc*

Then down to hell I took my way / For my true love's deliverance,
And rose again on the third day, / Up to my true love and the dance. *etc*

Then up to heaven I did ascend, / Where now I dwell in sure substance,
On the right hand of God, that man / May come unto the general dance. *etc*

58. The Twelve Dances of Christmas or Christmas mescolanza

♩ = 120 For the .... dance of Christmas my true love asked of me   12, 11, 10, 9, 8, 7, 6 ...

C   G   C   G drone

5 counts of bow then rise   4 hands over   3 steps under   2 lines back, and a pair of circles going round

C Am D   G   C   F   D   G   C F   C   G   C F C

Form pairs of couples facing pairs of couples in as many ranks of 4-people as will facing up or down the hall. **Start** left foot. **Play, sing and dance as a cumulative song**, starting each time through with the setting and turning, matching the declaration of the 'dance … asked of me', then doing the figures to match the relevant verses. The figures for the 3rd, 4th and 6th verses involve progressing past current opposites to face a new rank.

	Lyric sung (/ divides crotchets)	Ct	Figure danced
First chorus	**For the /**	up	
	first / dance of / Christ/mas my / true love / asked of / me / a	8	Set left and right Turn over left shoulder
Verse 1	**pair / of / circles / going / ro/u/nd / -**	8	(Within each minor set of 8) taking hands with partner and opposites to form **1** pair of circles each going 4 hands fully around to left.
Later choruses	**For the /**	up	
	2nd[etc] / dance of / Christ/mas my / true love / asked of / me / -	8	
2	**Two / lines / back, / and a** [Verse 1 as before]	4	(Within each minor set of 8) without holding hands 2 steps forward in **2** ranks to meet oncoming opposite both hands pressing at chest height then push back 2 steps into circle of 8
3	**Three / steps / under**	3	(Each individual) take **3** steps forward, downward-facing couples dip under arching-upcoming couples
4	**Four / hands / over**	3	Taking inside hands with partner and (within the downward-facing rank) downward-facing couples arch with **4** hands high over dipping upcoming couple
5	**Fi/ve / counts / of /** **bow / then / rise / -**	8	(Within verse) all bow to opposites for **5** counts (1 ¼ bars) then on last 3 counts of 8 count phrase (of 2nd bar) rise and take inside hands with partner.
6	**Six / between ne/ar misses**	3	(Within each minor set of 8) pull past opposite by left shoulder, **6** doing so by pulling on 2-hands and passing between two others.
7	**Seven / nods o/r kisses**	3	(Within each ranks of 4) the **3** who can nod to same sex corner on right, then all **4** kiss toward left check of opposite.
8	**Eight / left-hand / takings**	3	(Within each minor set of 8) **8** dancers take and shake 3 times the left hand of the opposite, and retain left hands.

John Gardiner-Garden, *The Christmas Carol Dance Book*, 2020

9	**Nine / right-hand / shakings**	3	(Within each minor set of 8) the **3** on each side who can, step right as they shake hands **3 times** with same-sex corner on right and retain hand.
10	**Ten-/finger / meetings**	3	(Within each pair of facing dancers) as each dancer claps all **10** fingers palm to palm with opposite 3 times.
11	**(E)leven / lively / greetings**	3	(Within each minor set of 8) each dancer waves with left hand to opposite, right hand to right diagonal (if someone there), left to opposite, so number of meetings is **4**, **3** and **4**.
12	**Twelve / stately / steppings**	3	(Within each rank) **4** dancers strut on alternate feet **3 times**

The idea for this dance came to me in December 2018. Having crafted more than 70 dances to go to Christmas Carols but having time enough at any one Christmas ball to dance only about 20, I try to program for each year's Christmas Carol Ball dances that were not danced at the preceding two ball, that is that hadn't been danced for 3 years… but nearly every year we have 'The Twelve Days of Christmas' (presented in next dance entry) requested and I oblige. After dancing that dance at the 2018 ball it occurred to me how neat it would be if the items that were being enumerated were the names of the dance figure about to be danced. It occurred to me that what people enjoy most in doing 'The Twelve Days of Christmas' was the singing while doing of cumulative actions with a succession of opposites and that we might be able to have the same fun with a dance in a different formation and a different lyric. For a different formation I thought a double-wide mesoclanze might be ideal as unlike a single circle it can fill the whole middle of the hall, as a ranks-of-4 face up in between ranks-of-4 facing down—and if the crowd or space is not sufficient for a series of columns the dance can work equally well with one 4-a-breast column. For the lyric I though how much fun it would be if what was being referred to was not presents-sent but figures-requested, so the dance becomes full of references to the dance art that sustains it, and the song being sung becomes the call for the dance. The first time you try the dance the rhythmic promptings might seem to come a bit late to function as a call as they are sung at the same time as performing the figure rather than announced before the figure, but after practicing the pairing of song and figures once or twice, dancers will come to associate the number sing at the beginning of a figure with the rhyming lyric and action that follows over the next few of counts, so the lyric, or at least anticipation of it, can become an effective call.

In this new dance I occasionally pay homage to the original lyric or original dance. For example, in 'dance 1' the words **pair / of** echo the original dance's **'Partridge'** and in the new dance **Fi/ve / counts / of / bow / then / rise** alludes not only to the bow you do in this new dance but also at that point in the old. The arching in this new dance also make us think a little about that most archetypic British Isle's Christmas-time dance, Sir Roger de Coverley. For three images of this dance happening under hanging Christmas garlands see my introductory section 'On dancing at Christmas'. Here is an image of it, with its characteristic arching, as 'drawn by Overend', in *The Illustrated London News* Christmas Number 1883, p.24:

59. The Twelve Days of Christmas

♩ = 120 For the .... day of Christmas my true love asked of me   12, 11, 10, 9, 8, 7, 6 ...

C   G   C   G drone

5 gold rings   4 calling birds   3 French hens   2 turtle doves and a partridge in a pear tree

C Am D   G   C   F   D   G   C F   C   G   C F C

Form a circle of as many couples as will, M facing along l.o.d., W against. **Start** r.f.. **Prepare** for setting, walking, clapping, capering and stomping. **Play, sing and dance as a cumulative song**, beginning each day with the setting and dancing all the figures up to that point. The figures for the 2nd, 3rd, 4th days involve progressions on to new partners.

On the ... day of Christmas	Set right and left.
My true love sent to me	Turn single over r.sh. with 4 walking steps.
A partridge in a pear tree	L.sh. gypsy whole way around with 8 steps.
2 turtle doves	Pass r.sh. (with eye contact – litting hands like bird wings) with 4 steps.
3 french hens	Pull l.h. past next with 3 steps.
4 calling birds	Pull r.h. past next with 3 steps.
(slowly) 5 gold rings	Reverance (W courtesy *while* M bow bending a knee and flourish a hand).
6 geese-a-laying	Clap l.h. with opposite 3 times.
7 swans-a-swimming	Clap r.h. with opposite 3 times.
8 maids a milking	Clap both hs with opposite 3 times.
9 ladies dancing	W caper with 3 (lady-like) kicks.
10 lords a leaping	M caper with 3 (lord-like) kicks.
11 pipers piping	Stamp own feet 3 times (as if a marching in a pipe band).
12 drummers drumming	Clap own hs 3 times.

Some see this carol originating in the coded-check-list of Christian doctrines popular in Renaissance times. As there are, however, many versions of the text (a French one having a gastronomic flavour) and as the tune is a similar to a 12th century French troubadour one, the carol might actually go back to Medieval games in which players have to recite all the items mentioned by others or forfeit. Christmas presents would have been an obvious subject of such a game as in those days celebrations extended from Christmas Day to the Feast of the Epiphany (marking when the Wise Men arrived with their gifts). Those who could afford it would give gifts on each day. Those who couldn't afford the gift giving could at least sing about it.

In writing a cumulative dance to go with this carol I was inspired by William Beck, who wrote one in a Sicilian formation in the 1980s. This single circle version is a lot easier and dancers can learn all the figures in one go upon walking through the 12th day - then dance from the first day. I've tried for figures which echo in some way the present of the day as well as to fit the beats allowed (which though usually 4, is for some gifts 3 and others 8). So turn single in the chorus as if dizzy with love, gypsy on day 1 as if walking around and staring at a partridge in a pair tree, pass r.shs (in what is effectively a ½ r.sh. gypsy) on day 2 as if a pair of coo-ing turtle doves, offer a reverance on day 5 worthy of 5 gold rings, caper on days 9 and 10 in the fashion of a lady dancing or lord leaping (perhaps just the W singing as they dance and just the men singing as they leap), stamp on day 11 as if a pipe major marching and clap on day 12 as if playing drummers or cymbals.

60. Unto Us a Child is Born

Form couples standing around a room holding inside hand with partner (W on r.side of M) and a candle in outside hand. **Start** l.f. and with only one couple having their candles lit, others with unlit candles on the periphery waiting to be greeted. **Prepare for** double and single steps, and reverences (bows). **Finish sequence** snowballing on to activate new dancers. **Play and dance** the 12-bar sequence **as many times as will**.

Unto us a boy is born!
King of all creation
Came he to a world forlorn,

The Lord of every
na...tion.

Cradled in a stall was he
With sleepy cows and asses;
But the very beast could see
That he all men
surpa...sses.

Herod then with fear was filled:
'A prince', he said , 'in Jewry!'
All the little boys he killed
At Bethlem in his
fu...ry.

Now may Mary's son, who came
So long ago to love us,
Lead us all with hearts aflame
Unto the joys
abo...ve us.

Omega and Alpha he!
Let the organ thunder,
While the choir with peals of glee
Doth rend the air
asu....nder.

A   Couples promenade in any direction with 2 double steps (ea. 2 bars long), starting l.f. and ending look out for opposite couple)

B   With <u>l.f.</u> double draw so close to a facing couple that you can <u>switch</u> from holding partner's inside hand <u>to holding opposites' hand</u>, i.e. each M can take opposite W's l.h. in his r.h.

C   Step back on r.f.
Reverence (low bow) to new partner, and as you rise <u>light (if unit) candle</u> held by new partners and turn back a little on former partner.

This carol is a loose translation of the Latin song 'Puer nobis nascitur'. This song was used in the medieval liturgy and was found in the 14th century German manuscript, the Moosburg Gradual, in a 15th century Trier manuscript and in the 16th century Finnish collection *Piae Cantiones*. The English translation used here was made by Percy Dearmer for the 1928 *Oxford Book of Carols*. Another commonly used translation is by G.R. Woodward.

Candle dances are, not surprisingly, common in many traditional dance genres. Arbeau, in his 1589 *Orchesographie*, recorded a beautiful candle mixer called 'Branle des Chandeliers' - danced with gentle allemande steps. The same style of steps is used in this dance. It was common in Renaissance courts for couples to take turn in dancing, and to be watched by all the other dancers. Snowballing dances which, like this one, start with one couple and finish with all dancing were less common but were also known. If the lights are dimmed this dance makes a pretty spectacle as flames flicker on more and more candles. When all the candles are lit you can either stop the dance or, better still, have couples continue to greet and change partners without the need to light each other's candle. If you want to have all candles lit by the time the 5th verse is sung and if dancers with lit candles always plan to greet dancers with unlit ones, then start with 1 in every 16 couples with lit candles. Give the task of extinguish the candles to someone for whom the day is special (eg the bridal couple, birthday boy or girl, the organiser) and either have them proceed around the hall blowing out the candles and someone else following collecting them in a basket, or have them stand still while everyone promenades around the room past them and the person collecting the candles.

John Gardiner-Garden, *The Christmas Carol Dance Book*, 2020

61. Veinticinco de Diciembre

♩ = 110

Form a Sicilian circle of as many couples-facing-couples as will. Start either foot. Prepare for walking and clapping. Finish sequence having progressed 4 places in original direction along or against the l.o.d.. Play and dance the bouncy 16-bar jig sequence as many times as will.

Veinticinco de diciembre,
Fum, fum, fum!

Veinticinco de diciembre,
Fum, fum, fum!

Nacidoha por nuestro amor,
El Niño Dios, el Niño Dios;
Hoy de la Virgen María
En esta noche tan fría
Fum, fum, fum!

Pajaritos de los bosques, *etc*
Vuestros hijos de coral
Abandonad, abandonad,
Y formad un muelle nido
A Jesús recién nacido, *etc*

Estrellitas de los cielos, *etc*
Que a Jesús miráis llorar
Y no lloráis, y no lloráis,
Alumbrad la noche oscura
Con vuestra luz clara y pura, *etc.*

Twenty-fifth day of December, *etc*
For the love of man is given
The holy infant, son of heaven;
Of the holy virgin springing,
Peace on earth and good will bringing,
etc

Birds that live with in the forest, *etc*
All you fledgling leave behind,
And seek the infant saviour kind.
Build, as well as you are able,
Downy nest to be his cradle, *etc*

Little stars up in the heavens, *etc*
If you see the baby cry,
O do not answer with a sigh!
Form the skies your radiance beaming,
Pierce the darkness with your gleaming,
etc.

A1   Giving inside hs to opposite, <u>lead out</u> with 4 steps <u>then</u>, with 3 steps accompanied by 3 claps, <u>turn in and about</u> and change to other inside hs.

A2   <u>Lead back</u> towards partner with 4 steps <u>then clap with partner r.h., l.h., both hs</u>, finishing clasping M's r.h. W's l.h. and turning to face opposite (so joined hs become inside hs).

B   1s (facing along the l.o.d., acw around double circle) go under an arch made by 2s (facing other way) to start a <u>dip and dive past 4 couples,</u> 4 steps for each arch - whether under or over.

Facing 5th couple <u>clap</u> r, l, both <u>with opposite</u> and clasping inside hs with opposite (M's r.h. W's l.h.) open out to side ready to lead out.

This is one of the few Spanish carols to be popular in the English-speaking world. The recurring 'Fum, fum, fum!' may be an imitation of an instrument - perhaps the strumming of a guitar. Here, to add to the dramatic Spanish flavour, we have complimented the refrain with clapping. As the dance sequence could happily be enjoyed through many repeats, we recommend following the original Spanish verses with English versions of the same verses, such as those offered here.

This fun dance combines something of the floor patterning of the such early English Country dances as 'Lull me beyond thee' and 'Hit and miss', with some of the clapping and waves you might expect in an Australian bushdance.

62. Verbum caro factum est

♩ = 180 [A] 2D f&b — M 2D b. *while* W 1D b. 1D f. — fine

Dm — C — Gm — F — Dm — B♭ — C — F

[B] 2D sideways l&r — M again l&r *while* guiding W from r. to l.

Dm — C — Dm — A — Dm — F — B♭ — C — F

[A var.] 2D sideways l&r — M again guide W across then all solo t.s. l. w. 2 D.

Dm — C — Gm — F — Dm — B♭ — C — F

Form a circle of as many couples as will. **Start** l.f. **Prepare for** doubles. **Finish sequence** with a double progression of partner. **Play and dance** the sequence **as many times as will.**

A (12 bars) <u>All go 2D forward to centre of circle</u> / Men 2D back *while* W go D b. then release hands &f. / Women 2D back *while* M go D f. to meet then &b. together.

B (8 bars) With 2 doubles <u>all go sideways left and right</u> / men again go D l&r *while* <u>guiding woman on right to his left</u>

A var. (12 bars) Repeat 8 bar B then in extra 4 bars all twirl solo acw to left with 2 D.

This hymn was printed in an anonymous Spanish music printed in Venice in 1556. The volume was entitled *Villancicos de diuersos Autores, a dos, y a tres, y a quatro, y ya a cinco bozes* but is commonly called the *Cancioneiro de Uppsala* as the only surviving copy of the work resided in the Uppsala University Library in Sweden. This hymn is said in the work's contents to be no. 33 and is often reported to be 39 but is actually on 35v-36 so I call it no.36. It is one of ten *Villancicos de Navidad* ('Carols for Christmas') which are said in the contents to be *A tres bozes* ('for 3 voices') but all are actually for *quato* ('four') voices. I'm indebted to Charis Messalina Helena de Valence for introducing me to this carol and to *I Progetti*, the chamber choir she directs, for singing this for dance at our Christmas carol balls.

In the choreography I have contrived to keep step and figure simple and hypnotic while incorporating variation, weight sharing and a progression. I've kept the steps simple by having them doubles throughout the whole dance for the men and women alike. I've kept the figures simple by having all movement on the in-out axis in the A part and on a sideways axis in the B and Avariant parts. I've contrived to make all hypnotic by having everyone constantly moving. I've created variation in the A by turning what could have been a simple into the middle and back into a more flower-like closing and opening action. I've created some weight sharing by giving the men in the B and A variant part the sensation of guiding the women across. I've worked into the sequence a double progression so each time you recommence you do so between two new neighbours. The final solo twirl to the left is to titillate and disorient all with a little dizziness just before all recommence.

Latin and Spanish	English translation
Verbum caro factum est **Porque todos os salvéis,** **porque todos os salvéis.**	And the word is made flesh for the salvation of us all. for the salvation of us all.
Y la Virgen le dezía: **Vida de la vida mia,** **Hijo mio, ¿qué os haría,** **Que no tengo en qué os echéis?** *Chorus*	And the Virgin spoke to Him: Life of my life, My son, what shall I do, having nothing in which to dress you? *Chorus*
O riquezas (temporales/terrenales), **¿No daréis unos pañales** **A Jesu que entre animales** **Es nasçido según véis?** *Chorus* etc.	O you the rich of this world, will you not give a swaddling cloth to Jesus, born amidst the beasts as you may behold? *Chorus* etc.

63. Vom Himmel Hoch, O Englein, Kommt!

Form a Sicilian circle of as many couples-facing-couples as will. Start either foot. Prepare for walking steps. Finish sequence having progressed as a couple one place in original direction (1s along l.o.d., 2s against). Play and dance the 14-bar jig sequence as many times as will.

Vom Himmel hoch, O Englein, kommt!	A	With 4 walking steps 1s promenade down the centre past opposite couples *while* 2s separate and go up outside
Eia, eia,		2s, with backs to 1s, take near inside hs and all swap sides with partner, W going under M's raised r.h., and about face to face same opposites from other directions (1s against l.o.d., 2s along l.o.d.) .
Susani, susani, susani! Kommt, singt und klingt, kommt, pfeift und trombt! *Hal le -lu jah, Hal le lu jah.*	B	As above but in reverse roles back to starting places.
Von Jesus singt und Maria.		Taking hs with original opposite couple, all go forward with 2 steps into centre of minor set and back with 2 steps
	C	Circle cw ½ way, then release neighbours hs and turn about as a couple (W under M's raised r.h.) to face new opposites.

Kommt ohne Instrumente nit.
- *Chorus 1* -
Bringt Lauten, Harfen, Geigen mit.
- *Chorus 2* -

Lasst hören euer Stimmen viel!
- *Chorus 1* -
Mit Orgel und mit Saitenspiel.
- *Chorus 2* -

Hier muss die Musik himmlisch sein
- *Chorus 1* -
Weil dies ein himmlisch' Kinderlein
- *Chorus 2* -

Sehr süss muss sein der Orgel Klang,
- *Chorus 1* -
Süss über allen Vögelsang
- *Chorus 2* -

Das Lautenspiel müss lauten süss,
- *Chorus 1* -
Davon das Kindlein schlafen müss.
- *Chorus 2* -

Singt Fried' den Menschen weit und breit,
- *Chorus 1* -
Gott Preis und Ehr' in Ewigkeit.
- *Chorus 2* -

This carol goes back to the 14th century when it was common in German churches for the priest at Christmas time to rock a cradle in front of the altar in time to the singing. In this context 'eia' means 'hush' and 'susani' is low German for 'suse Ninne' or 'sleep child.' The wonderful musical demands made in verses are captured well in this *Shorter New Oxford book of Carols'* translation:

Come angels come, from heaven appear *etc*
Come sing, come pipe, come trumpet here! *etc.*
Your instruments of music bring: *etc*
The lute and harp, and bowed string. *etc.*
Let strings and organ all agree *etc*
To weave a solemn harmony. *etc.*

Celestial music sound on high, *etc*
for here a heavenly Child doth lie! *etc.*
Your angel voices gently blend *etc*
In psalms and songs that have no end *etc.*
Let sweetest organ-tones be heard, *etc*
More sweet than any singing-bird *etc.*

With softest touch let lutes reply, *etc*
To soothe the Child with lullaby. *etc.*
Sing peace to men, where'er they be: *etc*
Sing praise to God eternally! *etc.*

This dance tries to capture the two seemingly incongruous images in the carol's lyric and melody - triumphant celebration on the one hand and gentle rocking on the other. Bold advances down the centre and joyous circling are thus alternated with tender under-arm turning as a couple.

John Gardiner-Garden, *The Christmas Carol Dance Book*, 2020

64. Walking in the air

Form couples in waist-shoulder hold basket. **Start** either foot. **Prepare for** walking steps and buzz-step basket. **Dance** sequence to 3rd part of movie music score (i.e. strains presented below) as many times as will. **Play** 2 bar intro. then ABCC as many times then 8-bar ending based on A strain.

Just 1st time	**Intro.** 8 counts	Full bow to partner.
Verse 1, 2, 3 or 4	**Aa** 8 counts	with 4 steps fall back; with 4 steps snowman (going back) wheels partner on right 3/4 acw (snowman back) to face along l.o.d.
	Ab 12 counts	with 8 steps wheel ¾ cw (snowman forward with left hand flying out) to end facing in / with 4 steps all forward to touch hands in grand circle
	Ac 8 counts	counterpart of above but without final going forward: with 4 steps fall back; with 4 steps snowman (going back) wheels corner on left 3/4 cw to face along l.o.d. /
	Ad 8 counts	with 8 steps wheel ¾ acw (snowman forward with right hand flying out) to end facing in and retaking inside hand of partner
Not Sung	**Ba1** 8 counts	find opposite couple and circle ½ cw /
	Ba2 8 counts	find new opp. couple and circle ½ cw
	Bb 16 counts	2h turn opposite cw ½ or 1½ into grand circle that goes to left
Bridge 1 or 2	**C** 16 counts	with 8 steps snowman (going back) wheels partner once acw and releases woman/child so they goes ahead into centre / women/children take hands in circle and arch *while* snowmen holding hs put their heads under the arch straight ahead to the left of their partner , rise and all form a grand basket with women/children's hands around snowmen's shoulders and snowmen's hands held around women/children's waist
	C variant 16 counts	with 8 buzz-step all turn the basket progressively quicker cw /continue to buzz-step the basket until the women/children who-will can fly with feet off the ground

Just last	**Ending**	Reprise the A action, but slowing as the snowman melts and end with a bow.
time	36 counts	
verse 1		

The arrangement for this dance is slightly different from that for the movie but all the same verses and bridges can be used.

For the first A and 'Ending' A:

Verse 1)
We're walking in the air
We're floating in the midnight sky
And everyone who sees us
greets us as we fly

For other As choose between (or sing on successive playing):

Verse 2)
I'm holding very tight
I'm riding in the midnight blue
I'm finding I can fly so high above with you

Verse 3)
Far across the world
The villages go by like trees
The rivers and the hills
The forests and the streams

Verse 4)
We're surfing in the air
We're swimming in the frozen sky
We're drifting over icy
Mountains floating by

For the C & C variant choose between:

Bridge 1)
Children gaze open mouth
Taken by surprise
Nobody down below believes their eyes

Bridge 2)
Suddenly swooping low
on an ocean deep Arousing of a mighty
monster from its sleep

'Walking in the Air''s lyrics and music of were written by Howard Blake in 1982 for the film *The Snowman*. The film was based on Raymond Brigg's 1978 children's book by the same name, in which a snowman comes to life and takes a boy on a flight to the North Pole, where they attend a snowman party, and meet Father Christmas. In the film the song was sung by chorister Peter Auty but he was accidently left out of credits and not reinstated by producers till 2002. The song became a seasonal favourite in many countries, but perhaps especially in Britain where it has been many times recorded (with Welsh chorister Aled Jones's 1985 recording reaching number 5 in the UK pop charts and with many people mistakingly thinking he was the voice on the film) and in Finland where it has been given Finnish lyrics and become a Christmas carol.

I attempted to create a dance that be enjoyed either by a man with a woman as a partner or by a snowman with a young person as a partner, and so that the dance is not too confusing or too dangerous for a young person you are nearly always holding on to someone's hand—the only excepting being the moment when the women or young person goes in to take hands in a ring in the centre, and thought that trapise-transfer moment might be fun, and as the arches are raised on the inside give an insentive for the snowmen to dip down under the raised soon after the lyric says 'flying-low'.

In my dance I attempted to capture in the A part the sensation of taking off without doing any one action too long in one direction. In this part I am also keen that the man's free hand can always take the hand of the partner or person beside them from below. In the B part I was keen to capture the sensation of wandering the skys, and use it as an opportunity to change snowmen. In the C part I was keen to capture the sensation of flying—creating an opportunity for any light partner that will, being securely held by others, to let their feet leave the ground as the basket rotates ever faster. I propose you divide the 4 bars of the C variant between 4 counts of getting the buzz step working, 4 counts of all becoming as light as possible, 4 counts of willing-feet leaving the ground and 4 counts of setting back to a normal buzz step.

If with vocal accompaniment, I suggest doing the dance 4 times, in the
1st playing singing Verse 1) and Bridge 1)
2nd playing singing Verse 2) and Bridge 2)
3rd playing singing Verse 3) and Bridge 1)
4th playing singing Verse 4), Bridge 2) and a reprise of Verse 1).

John Gardiner-Garden, *The Christmas Carol Dance Book*, 2020

65. We Three Kings

Form a trio of W-M-W facing a trio of M-W-M. Start M l.f., W r.f.. Prepare for travelling waltz steps. Finish sequence having progressed in original trio formation in original direction against or along l.o.d. to face new trio. Play and dance the 32-bar waltz sequence as many times as will.

We three Kings of Orient are;
Bearing gifts we traverse afar,
field and fountain,
moor and mountain,
following yonder
star… O
Star of wonder,
star of night,
Star with royal
beauty bright
Westward leading,
still proceeding
Guide us to thy
perfect light.

A1	With 4 waltz steps do-si-do opposite r.sh.
A2	All take 4 waltz steps to travel cw ½ way around minor set.
B	M all turn about over r.sh. to give r.h. to W behind.
	Chain past (M acw W cw around set) to give l.h. to next.
	Pull past on l.h. to give r.h. to next.
	Pull past r.h. to give l.h. to next (same as first person in chain).
C1	W join r.hs, release l.h., and take 8 waltz steps to star once *while* M
&2	take 4 waltz steps to travel alone ½ acw around circle, about turn and take original r.side W's l.h. in their r.h., then take 4 waltz steps to travel back to place with W.
D	With 6 waltz steps fall out into holding hs in circle (W wheel a little back M forward) and circle once left, finishing facing original direction ready to pull through.
	With 2 waltz steps pass opposite r.sh. to face new opposite.

Born a King on Bethlehem's plain
Gold I bring to crown him again
King forever, ceasing never
Over us all to reign.
- *Chorus* -

Frankincense to offer have I,
Incense owns a Deity nigh;
Prayer and praising, all men raising,
Worship him God most high.
- *Chorus* -

Myrrh is mine; its bitter perfume
Breathes a life of gathering gloom;
Sorrowing, sighing, bleeding, dying,
Sealed in the stone cold tomb.
- *Chorus* -

Glorious now behold him arise,
King and God and Sacrifice.
Halleluia, Halleluia,
Earth to heaven replies.
- *Chorus* -

John Henry Hopkins Jr. wrote this carol for a Christmas pageant for the General Theological Seminary in New York City in 1857 and published it in his *Carols, Hymns and Songs* in 1865. The legend of the 3 kings goes back at least to a 6th century Armenian tale in which Melkon, king of the Persians, brought myrrh, aloes, rare fabrics and books written and sealed by the finger of God; Gaspar, king of the Hindus, brought nard, cinnamon and incense; and Balthasar, king of the Arabs, brought gold, silver, sapphires and pearls. The legend became popular in Europe, the gifts being simplified and names becoming Melchior, Caspar and Balthazar. In the 12th century 3 perfectly preserved bodies found under a church near Milan were thought to be those of the kings and were moved to Cologne Cathedral for veneration. The star in the story has been thought to reflect memory of an astronomical event such as a comet's arrival or a planetary conjunction - there being several in the last decade BC.

This dance closely follows the carol's storyline. You, the kings, introduce yourselves by do-si-do-ing. Bearing gifts you travel solo around the circle. Following the star, you weave from one hand to the next in a chain. The women make the star of wonder, but are joined by the men to make a much bigger 'Star with royal beauty bright'. Leading westward you circle clockwise and, still proceeding, you circle some more. Guided to thy perfect light, you pull through in a straight line along or against the l.o.d. to meet new opposites.

66. Wish You a Merry Christmas

Form couples in a circle broken at two opposite points. **Start** M l.f., W r.f.. **Prepare for** travelling and turning waltz steps. **Finish sequence** with 2 couples having left the now reduced-in-size broken circle. **Dance** the 16-bar brisk waltz until no one is left in the circle and all are waltzing around the outside. **Play** tune **as many times as will and finish with A strain.**

We wish you a merry Christmas,
We wish you a merry Christmas,
We wish you a merry Christmas,
and a happy New Year
Glad tidings we bring

To you and your kin;
Glad tidings for Christmas
And a happy New Year!
Oh, bring us a figgy pudding,
Oh, bring us a figgy pudding,
Oh, bring us a figgy pudding,
and a cup of good cheer.
- Chorus -

We won't go until we get some,
We won't go until we get some,
We won't go until we get some,
so bring some out here
- Chorus -

We all know that Santa's coming,
We all know that Santa's coming,
We all know that Santa's coming,
And soon will be here
- Chorus -

We wish you a merry Christmas
We wish you a merry Christmas
We wish you a merry Christmas
And a happy New Year

We wish you a merry Christmas
We wish you a merry Christmas
We wish you a merry Christmas
And a happy New Year

A   All circle left with 8 waltz steps, semi-circles following lead of M on far left trace a circle around floor.

B   *While* others circle back to right with 8 waltz steps, l.h. end couples, break off, go in with 2 waltz steps
take hs as group of 4 dancers and circle left with 2 waltz steps.
½ 2h turn opp. to exchange places with 2 waltz steps and…
with W now on her partner's left, circle left again with 2 waltz steps.

A   *While* others repeat semi-circles following each other going left (cw) around floor, those now in the centre pull their partner into a ballroom hold and waltz acw round the inside of the circling dances and out through the first gap they find.

B   Repeat above B part - sending new l.h. end couple in for circle, swap with opposite, circle and ballroom hold with partner.

As mentioned earlier, the heirs to the wassailers were the waits, singers licensed to announce the hours of day or night, to greet visiting dignitaries, to enliven weddings for the well-off and, at Christmas time, to make the holiday merrier by serenading citizens on frosty nights - hoping, like their wassailing forbears, to receive a coin, a bit of fig pudding, a sip of ale or some other treat, in return. This carol is one of theirs.

This dance has the rare character of being a reverse snowball – everyone starts dancing together but slowly all leave the formation. It is a wonderful way to end an evening - combining the sense of community offered by holding hands in a circle with the civility of interacting with opposites. It combines the game quality of trying to escape from the centre with the romance of a waltz with your partner. If there is a large crowd and you don't want to have to repeat verses to many times, start with several circles of 20 or so couples. Once you have waltzed out of your circle, go on to waltz the hall. As others join so the radius of each broken circle (or pair of semi-circles, depending how you want to think of it) will shrink - thus allowing more room for the free waltzing. Return to 'We wish you' verse for all to waltz the hall together, open out facing in and take hs in a grand circle, then sing the verse again so all (while holding hs in circle) can go into the centre with 4 waltz steps and retire with 3 waltz steps and a bow.

John Gardiner-Garden, *The Christmas Carol Dance Book*, 2020

67. What Child is This?

Form a circle of as many couples as will, M facing along W against l.o.d.. **Start** either foot. **Prepare for** quick waltz travelling steps. **Finish sequence** either with same partner or having progressed on to new partner (M along l.o.d, W against). **Play and dance** this 32-bar waltz like sequence **as many times as will.**

What Child is this who, laid to rest	A1	With 4 brisk waltz steps release r.hs to sweep them up, out and around in wide arc and rejoin below l.hs, release l.hs in a wide arc and rejoin below r.hs.
On Mary's lap is sleeping?		Repeat arcs.
Whom angels greet with anthems sweet	A2	Taking r.h. in r.h over l.h. in l.h, M turns W once over her r.sh. with another 4 waltz steps to peek-a-boo then back over her l.sh.
While shepherds watch are keeping?		M raises joined hs, turns W twice over her r.sh. to finish r.sh. to r.sh, and lowers l.hs to spy partner through a r.sh. window.
This, this is Christ the King,	B1	In this window hold turn as a couple cw once around.
Whom shepherds guard and angels sing;		M raises joined hs again, turn W thrice over her l.sh. to finish l.sh. to l.sh., and then lowers r.hs to make a l.sh. window.
Haste, haste, to bring him laud,	B2	In this window hold turn as a couple acw once around.
The Babe, the Son of Mary.		M raises joined hs and turns W twice over l.sh. to finish facing partner l.hs joined over r.hs, then release r.hs, pull past l.sh. and reach out with r.h. to go palm to palm with new partner.

Why lies he in such mean estate,
Where ox and ass are feeding?
Good Christians, fear, for sinners here
The silent word is pleading.
Nails, spear shall pierce him through,
The cross be borne for me, for you.
Hail, hail the word made flesh,
The Babe, the won of Mary.

So bring him incense, gold and myrrh,
Come peasant, king to own him;
The king of kings salvation brings,
Let loving hearts enthrone him.
Raise, raise a song on high,
The virgin sings her lullaby.
Joy, joy for Christ is born,
The babe, the son of Mary.

The words of this carol were written in 1865 by William Chatterton Dix, whose father had so loved poetry that he gave his son a middle name in honour of poet Thomas Chatterton. William himself, though a manager of a marine insurance company in Glasgow, so loved poetry that he wrote 40 hymns. He set this one, 'The Manger Throne', to the 16th century tune *Greensleeves*. Other seasonal lyrics have also been set to this tune - including an old English song which begins 'The old year now has fled' and for which there is a dance in this collection under that heading. The original text to the melody goes:

> Alas my love, ye do me wrong
> to cast me off discurteously:
> And I have loved you so long,
> Delighting in your companie.
> *Greensleeves was all my joy*
> *Greensleeves was my delight:*
> *Greenslees was my heart of gold,*
> *And who but my Ladie Greensleeves.*

This dance, replete as it is with romance and entwined arms, probably echos less the words of Dix' 19th century hymn and more those which originally went to the 16th century tune. Indeed, if you sing the original song while doing the dance you end up singing about being wronged and casting off discourteously when pushing off each others hands, about the love borne while viewing each other under the peek-a-boo arches, and 'Greensleeves' as you intertwined raised arms, dangling sleeves before each others eyes.

68. & 69 Where is Santa? 1&2

♩ = 110

[Musical notation with markers 1, 2, 3, 4 above the staff; marked "As a round", 4/4 time]

1. Form 4 concentric circles of as many as will, no partner necessary. **Start** l.f.. **Prepare** for walking steps. **Play and dance** the 16-bar round to the tune of 'Frère Jacques' **as many times as will**.

Where is Santa?	A	Take 8 steps to <u>circle left</u>.
Where is Santa?		
Here I am.	B	Take 8 steps to <u>turn</u> solo <u>over l.sh.</u> with hs waving in the air.
Here I am.		
Merry, merry Christmas.	C	Take 8 steps to <u>circle right</u>.
Merry, merry Christmas.		
Ho, Ho, Ho.	D	Take 8 steps to <u>turn</u> solo <u>over r.sh.</u> with arms out front at waist height
Ho, Ho, Ho.		as if around a big belly.

2. Form square sets of 4 couples, i.e. quadrille formation, couples in waist-shoulder hold with partner and numbered acw. **Start** l.f.. **Prepare for** walking steps. **Play and dance** the 16-bar round to the tune of Frère Jacques **as many times as will,** finishing either all at once or, as in the canon, one couple after another.

Where is Santa?	A	With 8 steps <u>wheel acw</u> (W forward, M back).
Where is Santa?		
Here I am.	B	With 4 steps <u>retire</u> and 4 steps <u>advance</u>.
Here I am.		
Merry, merry Christmas.	C	With 8 steps <u>wheel cw</u> (M forward).
Merry, merry Christmas.		
Ho, Ho, Ho.	D	With 8 steps <u>lead through</u>, parting to around neighbours back to
Ho, Ho, Ho.		place (once underway, linking on with wheeling neighbours).

Here are two possible dances (a very simple one and a much more challenging one) to do to a 4 part round, where each part has 8 counts - such as this one to the tune of 'Frère Jacques'. The first dance is the simplest and matches the words of the song better - with the miming on the second and fourth parts. The second dance is an irresistible variant on Pat Shaw's famous 3-part canon 'Round Pond'. Although this dance is nothing more than 4 simple figures, once canonised the figures you dance dove-tail perfectly into the figures your neighbours are dancing - particularly if everyone gives weight when wheeling to create a central point around which you can go briskly forward or backward with just 8 steps and particularly if W when wheeling or leading through have their free r.h. raised so the neighbouring M can easily swing his l.h. around her waist and she slip her r.h. onto his l.sh. when they need to dovetail a caste and wheel (or wheel and caste). Indeed, you will discover that you end up doing 2 successive dovetailed figures so once taken you don't need to relinquish straight away the waist-shoulder hold with your neighbour. Once mastered and underway it is indeed hard to stop! Decide beforehand on what signal the first couple to start will stop dancing - and then allow the round to unravel, with the other couples stopping 8 steps apart - the last couple casting around stationary corners.

John Gardiner-Garden, *The Christmas Carol Dance Book*, 2020

70. While Shepherd Watch their Flocks

♩ = 110 [A]

[B] | Intro.

C   G⁷   Am   F   C   G   C   D   G   C

F   C   G   Am⁷   E⁷   Dm   G   C

Form a circle of any number of couples holding hs, though 6 couples is ideal. **Start** l.f.. **Prepare** to use a slow, slow, quick, quick, quick pattern on alternate feet (like a pavan but with no closure) throughout the dance. **Finish sequence** having completed a double progression, M acw W cw. **Play and dance** the 16-bar pavan-like sequence **as many times as will**, but **if a circle of 6 couples**, dance sequence **6 times** (once for each verse) to enable all to arrive back with original partner in original place.

While Shepherds watch their flocks by night All seated on the ground,	A	All <u>circle left</u> with a slow left, right and then a quick double or chassé starting with l.f. Continue circling with a slow right, left and then a quick double or chassé starting with r.f.
The angel of the Lord came down And glory shone around.	B	All go <u>in</u> with slow left and right, then release neighbour. With double step, <u>M swap partner under</u> his <u>raised r.h.</u> <u>Out</u> with slow right and left, then release partner and take near hs with neighbour. With double <u>M swap new W under</u> his <u>raised l.h.</u>

'Fear not,' said he, for mighty dread
had seized their troubled mind,
'Glad tidings of great joy I bring
To you and all man-kind'.

'To you in David's town this day
Is born of David's line
The Savior who is Christ the Lord,
And this shall be the sign.

The heav'nly babe you there shall find
To human view displayed.
All meanly wrapped in swathing bands
And in a manger laid.'

Thus spoke the seraph and forth-with
Appeared a shining throng
Of angels praising God, who thus
Addressed their joyful song:

'All glory be to God on high
And on the earth be peace!
Goodwill henceforth from heav'n to men
Begin and never cease'.

This carol was published in 1696 by Nahum Tate, a distinguished Irish writer and poet who lived in England in the late 17th early 18th century (co-authored a metrical version of the Psalms and re-wrote Shakespeare's King Lear to give it a happy ending). The text is so close to the scriptural Christmas story that it became the first carol to gain official approval in the Church of England - being included in the 1700 *Supplement to the New Version of the Psalms*. The tune to which it is most often sung is 'Winchester Old', a psalm tune that goes back at least as far as Este's *Psalter* of 1592. Richard Storrs Willis set the text to an aria from George F. Handel's 'Cyrus', 1728. The dance works to either melody, so long as the tune is not rushed.

This dance features 16th-century pavan footwork sequence without closing after each step (as was common in the Italian dance of earlier centuries). Rather than taking a full single left (rising and falling as feet come together), single right and close, then double left, right, left, and close, this dance uses a simple step left, step right, and 3 quick steps left, right, left - essential the same pattern but in half the time. This step is used whether circling left (miming the shepherd watching over the sheep), or chaining. Although the dance can work for any number of couples in a circle, 6 times through the dance affords 6 couples the opportunity to dance with all possible partners twice, the first time while progressing to the other side of the circle, the second time on the homeward half of the circle.

71. White Christmas

Form couples in high promenade hold **Start** right foot. **Prepare for** 1 *chassé* step (i.e. 1-2-3-lift) per bar. **Dance** sequence as many times as will, M progress along l.o.d. ea. time but only kiss W every 2nd time. **Play** the signature Irving Berlin tune as many times as will.

A1	I'm dreaming of a	*Chassé* right forward then left sideways along l.o.d.
	white Christmas	*Chassé* right back then again left sideways
	Just like the ones I used to know... Where the	Repeat
B	treetops glisten... and	Raise hs and M goes behind W as she goes across in front to look at each other under raised left hands, then back to look under raised right hands
	children listen to	With hands still raised M turns W turn over her right shoulder to momentary form a window through which the dancers can look at each other over their right shoulder then, lowering his right hand, turns her back over her left into back skater's hold
	hear .... sleigh bells in the	With 2 *chassés* wheel cw about, M forward W backward and open out in wave, giving left hand to new partner while momentarily retaining right hand with old partner
	snow...	With 2 *chassés* or 4 slow walking steps left hand turn new partner into high promenade hold.
A2	I'm dreaming of a white Christmas with every Christmas card I write... May your	Repeat A1 of dance
C	days be merry and brigh[pause]t... and may all your Christmases be white	Repeat B1 of dance, but with the pause on 'bright' in bar 3 dancers kiss each other through the window careful not to lose timing on left chassé into wave.

I wrote the above dance in about 2002 but didn't put it in the first edition of my Christmas Carol Book, didn't put it on any Ball program that I recall and only led it once before letting it fall into disuse. I subsequently lost track of my notes and only found them again in 2015. I included the notes in the 2015 edition of my *Odd Delights* but did not get to reintroduce the dance to local dancers till 2017. It was then so well received we put it in our Christmas Carol Ball that year, and it was requested again in 2019. I think its now a favourite among people who like couples dancing.

The scmaltzy Christmas song to which my dance is set was written by Irving Berlin for the 1941 movie *Holiday Inn*. Berlin's assignment was to write a song about each of the major holidays for the year. Bing Crosby, who was to star in the movie with Fred Astaire, heard Berlin's 'White Christmas' at a working session in 1941, thought it great and introduced it to the public on his radio show on 25 December, 1941. He recorded the song in May 1942 and *Holiday Inn* was released in August that year. The piano music reproduced below was also released that year. The song became very popular with the war-time public and was a favourite when Crosby toured troops. It became the biggest-selling single of all time and remained so until 1998. So popular was it that the 1942 master recording became damaged through frequent use and the song had to be rerecorded in 1947. The success led in 1954 to the movie *White Christmas*—staring Crosby and Danny Kaye (Astaire declined the role).

To give a sense of gliding effortlessly on ice I have choreographed the entire dance with an unchanging pattern of glide-together-glide-life 'chassés' on alternate feet. I have also tried to bring out something of the lyric in the choreography. When in the first hard of A you are 'dreaming of a white Christmas' I suggest you imagine you are on blades as you slide forward, sideways, backward, sideways. When in the second half of A you are reminiscing about 'Just like the ones I used to know' or 'with every Christmas card' you do what was just done again. When in the first 2 bars of B you the 'treetops glisten' or the 'days be merry' you raise you hands high and as the woman steps somewhat in place the man goes behind her to regard her from her side, then back to regard her from his side. When in the second 2 bars of B1 the 'children listen' you turn the woman about as if listening out for each other under raised left hand, and when that bar comes around in B2 and you hear the slight pause on 'bright' you can kiss under the arch—either the a man the woman on her right cheek, or, if the woman wants to and can turn sufficiently, kiss mutually. With the third 2 bars of B there is no clear echo of the lyric, but if you time the opening out at the end of the wheel well, every dancer on the floor will momentarily be holding hands in a wave, right hand to past partner, left hand to future one, exactly as you go into the last 2 bars, which are the left hand turn with the new.

If you don't want the dance to be progressive, after the back-skater's hold wheel, the man in the last 2 bars pirouette's the woman cw under his raised right hand and then resumes the high promenade hold with this partner.

It's possible that you can start the dance with just 1 couple on the floor, doing the non-progressive sequence twice (to one singing of the whole song) the second time not only kissing and after the wheel instead of pirouetting opening out and giving left hand to a new partner to bring them onto the floor. When all are 'snowballed' onto the floor, you can do the group dance described above with a momentary full-circle 'wave' before the progression.

Below is a vintage image of skating on a frozen pond together with a reproduction from original in hand of the 1942 piano score which our pianist Sally Taylor uses and other musicians join in on when we are dancing the dance in scene.

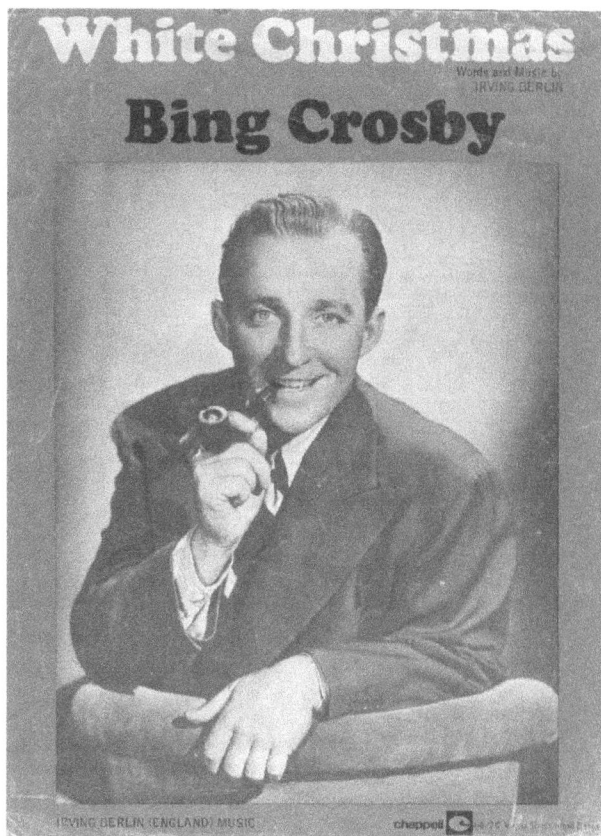

John Gardiner-Garden, *The Christmas Carol Dance Book*, 2020

WHITE CHRISTMAS

Words and Music by

IRVING BERLIN

See back page for
Introduction and Verse

REFRAIN
Slowly with expression

VOICE

PIANO

I'm dream-ing of a WHITE CHRIST-MAS Just like the

mf - f

C6   F6   C   B   C   Dm7   F#7   G7   F

ones I used to know, _____ Where the tree - tops glis-ten And

G7   Dm7   G7   C   Cmaj7   C6   Dm7   G7   C   Cmaj7   C7

chil - dren lis-ten to hear sleigh bells in the snow. _____

F   Fm6   C6   F   C   Bm   D7   Dm7   Fmaj7   Em7   Dm7

John Gardiner-Garden, *The Christmas Carol Dance Book*, 2020

I'm dream-ing of a WHITE CHRIST-MAS;

Cmaj7 G9 C6 G7 C6 F6 C B C Dm7 F#7 G7

With ev-'ry Christ-mas card I write_____ May your

F G7 Dm7 G7 C Cmaj7 C6 Dm7 G7

days be mer-ry and bright_____ And may all your

C Cmaj7 C7 F Fm C C#o

1 **2**

Christ-mas-es be white._____ white._____

Dm7 Em G7 C Cmaj7 Dm7 G7 C Dm7 C

FINE

INTRODUCTION AND VERSE

Slowly with expression

mf
ad lib.

Fm   C   C#o   Dm7   Em   G7   C   Dm7   C

The sun is shin-ing, the grass is green, The o - range and palm trees sway. There's

mf con al voce

Dm7   G7   Em7   C   G7   Dm7 G7   C6   C#o

nev-er been such a day in Bev-er-ly, Hills, L. A. But it's De-cem-ber the twen-ty-

Dm7   G9   Em7 Am7 Dm7   G9   C6   Fm6   G7   Dm7 G7

- fourth, _____ And I am long-ing to be _ up north. _____

Back to Refrain

accel. e rit.

Cmaj9   C6   Am6   B7   F#m7 B7 Em   Dm7   G7

Printed in Great Britain by Symphony Reproductions 60-70 Roden Street Ilford Essex IG1 2AQ

John Gardiner-Garden, *The Christmas Carol Dance Book*, 2020

Medleys

Having now offered the tunes, lyrics and instructions for all the individual dances in this book, I might note that many different sorts of medleys are also possible.

One type of medley is a straight-forward joining together in series some tunes and their dances as presented in this book. Ideally the dances would potentially involve the same number of dancers—for example, **A five-couple dance medley** can be made out of **Good King Wenceslas** and **Angelus ad Virginem**. To transition between these dances the couple who would normally go into the middle at the end of the 5th playing/dancing of 'Good King Wenceslas' join the others in slipping the circle on the periphery and is thus ready for 'Angelus ad Virginem'.

Another type of medley is the joining together of some tunes in this book, but using them as a setting for a new purpose. For example, **A medley of carols in 3/4** such as that which follows can be very useful. It can be played as background music when guests arrive (and some arrivals may wish to warm up waltzing to the music). It can be the setting for a dance game mid-way through the evening, be it one of the 19th century cotillon dance games I described in Volume VIII and X of my *Dancing through the Ages* books, or the **Waltz futsal** I describe in the 2020 edition of my *Dance Delights* and which we greatly enjoyed at our 2019 Christmas ball. It can also be used at the end of the evening for a free farewell couple's waltz—particularly if you end with 'We wish you a Merry Christmas'.

Silent Night x n.

Tomorrow shall be my dancing day x n.

We three kings x n.

We wish you a merry Christmas x n.

A third type of medley is joining together tunes not presented in this book (and there are hundreds in living non-English-speaking tradition) and using it as a setting for a new tailored choreography. Here is one such medley of tunes/dances we have enjoyed at our Christmas Carol Ball in Canberra. To three Christmas tune in a piano score from 1940s Sweden which our pianist Sally Taylor had and was keen to play I set versions of three original dances I had or have since published elsewhere—two in 2005 *Lost Dances of Earthly Delights* Volume 2 and one in my 2020 *Dance Delights*. We debuted the medley in 2019 and perhaps I might add it here as dance no.72: **Julpotpurri**.

John Gardiner-Garden, *The Christmas Carol Dance Book*, 2020

72. Julpotpurri ('A Christmas medley')

Form couples in ballroom hold. **Start** man left foot woman right foot free. **Prepare** for waltz, running, balance and draw steps. **Dance** as many times as will. **Play** the medley, as arranged below, of *Nu är det jul igen* ('Now it's Christmas again'), *Höga berg och djupa dalar* ('High mountains and deep valleys') and *Och jungfrun hon gar i dansen* ('O maiden she goes dancing'), *Hej, tomtegubbar* ('Hey Santa Claus') and *Nu ha vi ljus I vårt hus* ('Now we have light here in our house'). Play the suit once through to do dance twice through, or twice through to dance the dance four times.

John Gardiner-Garden, *The Christmas Carol Dance Book*, 2020

	To *Nu är det jul igen* ('Now it's Christmas again') once through with all internal repeats do my **Dance 1**, a version of **Conjuring L'amour** (*Lost Dances* Vol. 2, Country 12)		
A1	Nu är det jul igen Och nu är det jul igen Och julen varar väl till påska	Now it's Christmas again And now it's Christmas again And Christmas lasts well till Easter	With joined hands leading take <u>2 step draws along l.o.d. then</u> with 3 quick steps (1 <u>waltz</u> step) tum <u>cw 1/2 about (M backwards) and stomp</u> twice, finishing in exchanged places and other foot free (M's l.f., Ws r.f. free).
A2	*Repeat*	*Repeat*	With <u>shoulders leading, take 2 step draws along l.o.d.,</u> then 3 quick steps <u>tum cw 1/ 2 about (M again going backwards) and stomp twice,</u> finishing on original side with original starting foot free.
B1	Det var inte sant Det var inte sant För däremellan kommer fasta	That was not true That was not true Because in the middle there is Lent,	With 3 waltz steps, open out into holding inside hs <u>and travel forward along l.o.d. way balancing to face partner and away, then with inside foot (M's r.f., Ws l.f.) step towards partner and on next beat clap free outside hs</u> (M's l.h. with Ws r.h.).
B2	*Repeat*	*Repeat*	<u>Repeat</u> B1 ending still holding partner on inside hand <u>but in last bar</u> **(transition)** <u>instead of clapping free outside hs at end put free outside hand on own hip</u> (M's l.h. Ws r.h.).
	To *Höga berg och djupa dalar* ('High mountains and deep valleys') once through do my do my **Dance 2**, a version of first half of **Holiday Holubiec** (*Dance Delights*, 2020) with running steps —for two further verses see piano score.		
A	Höga berg och djupa dalar, här är vännen som migbehagar. Hej hopp, min lilla sockertopp, vi ska dansa tills solen rinner opp.	High mountains and deep valleys, here is the friend who pleases me. Hi ho, my little sweet one, we will dance until the rising sun.	<u>With 12 running steps man twirls partner cw x1 or x1 under his raised right hand</u> (inside hands). <u>With 12 running steps M bends or drops to knee and lassoos the W once acw about him, then rises</u>
B	Hej hopp, min sköna! Nu Vi ska dansat i det gröna.	Hi ho, my beautiful! Now We'll be dancing in the green.	<u>With 12 running steps M 'throws' W onto his left arm taking W's l.h. behind her back in his l.h. and W placing her r.h. on the man's l.sh. and together they wheel acw</u> (i.e. M f. W b.)
	Repeat	*Repeat*	<u>With 12 running steps and without letting go of the joined l.hs, the woman casts quickly out and goes behind the man to his right side where he puts his r.h. under her left arm around her waist to there take her r.h. and wheel acw as a couple (M back W forward) until both facing into circle then</u> **(transition)** <u>M turning over his l.sh. to face along l.o.d. W against l.o.d. holding l.h. in l.h. while W prepares to change weight in order to start next sequence with left foot free,</u> same as man.

<table>
<tr><td></td><td colspan="3">To *Och jungfrun hon gar i dansen* ('O maiden she goes dancing') once through
do my **Dance 3**, a version of **Vulgarian Salutations** (*Lost Dances* Vol. 2, Village 2)
—for four further verses see piano score</td></tr>
<tr><td>A</td><td>Och jungfrun hon går i dansen med röda gullband.</td><td>O maiden she goes dancing with red golden ribbons</td><td>Take r.hs *while* taking balance step left, take l.hs. *while* taking balance step right, then retaining l.hs wide l.h. turn each other with 2 waltz steps</td></tr>
<tr><td></td><td>*Repeat*</td><td>*Repeat*</td><td>With another 2 waltz steps complete l.h. turn and turn W once about over her l.sh., then with the next 2 bars of waltz music clap r, l, both, make a little jump back, and take 2hs.</td></tr>
<tr><td>B</td><td>Dem binder hon om sin kärastes arm,</td><td>She ties them around her sweetheart's arm</td><td>Leaning back balance each way by stepping left and swinging r.f. across, stepping right and swinging l.f. across, then with 2 waltz steps 2h tum once around.</td></tr>
<tr><td></td><td>*Repeat*</td><td>*Repeat*</td><td>Balance directly forward towards partner to kiss, backwards away from partner, then on last 2 bars (**transition**) if *wanting to repeat whole sequence with same partner* M pulls W into ballroom hold on his right side by letting go with his right hand and turning her 3/4 acw under his left hand as she comes towards him *or if wanting to repeat whole sequence with new partner* pull past partner by r.sh. and take next, by most direct means, in ballroom hold.</td></tr>
<tr><td></td><td colspan="3">To *Hej, tomtegubbar* ('Hey Santa Claus') one through with internal repeat of A
repeat my Dance 1.</td></tr>
<tr><td>A1</td><td>Hej, tomtegubbar, slån i glasen och låt oss lustiga vara!</td><td>Hey, Santa Claus, fill your glasses and let's be jolly together.</td><td rowspan="4">As for the version the first half of **Holiday Holubiec** offered earlier.</td></tr>
<tr><td>A2</td><td>*Repeat*</td><td>*Repeat*</td></tr>
<tr><td>B</td><td>En liten tid vi leva här, med mycket möda och stort besvär.</td><td>Our time is brief upon the earth, with troubles many and little mirth.</td></tr>
<tr><td>A3</td><td>As in A1</td><td>As in A1</td></tr>
<tr><td></td><td colspan="3">To *Nu ha vi ljus här i vårt hus* ('Now we have light here in our house')
twice through but without internal repeats
repeat my Dance 2 & 3—for other verse see piano score</td></tr>
<tr><td>1A

1B</td><td>Nu ha vi ljus här i vårt hus,
julen är kommen hopp tralalala!
Barnen i ring dansa omkring, dansa omkring.
Granen står så grön och grann i stugan.
Granen står så grön och grann i stugan.
Tralalalala, tralalalala, tralalalala, lala!</td><td colspan="2">Now we have light here in our house,
Christmas has come, hey tralalala!
The kids in the ring dance around, dance around.
The Christmas tree is so green and magnificent in the cottage.
The Christmas tree is so green and magnificent `in the cottage.
Tralalalala, tralalalala, tralalalala, lala!</td><td>As for the version of **Conjuring L'amour** offered earlier.</td></tr>
</table>

2A	Kom, lilla vän, kom nu igen!	Come, little friend, come now!	As for the version
	Dansa kring granen, hopp, tralalala!	Dance around the Christmas tree, he, tralalala!	of **Vulgarian**
	Glädjen är stor. Syster och bror,	The joy is great. Sister and brother, sister and	**Salutations**
	syster och bror,	brother,	offered earlier.
2B	pappa, mamma, alla gå i dansen,	dad, mom, everyone come to the dance	
	pappa, mamma, alla gå i dansen.	dad, mom, everyone come to the dance.	
	Tralalalala, tralalalala, tralalalala, lala!	Tralalalala, tralalalala, tralalalala, lala!	

The three-way relationship between Christmas, singing and dance, though largely lost in most English-speaking countries, has not been lost in many non-English-speaking ones. For example in Sweden, from where the songs in the above medley come, there has been a strong continuing tradition of communal dancing while singing either around a midsummer pole or in winter Christmas tree. *Nu är det jul igen* and *Höga berg och djupa dalar* are two song that are still so used today. *Och jungfrun hon gar i dansen* is another century old Swedish song that was traditionally used for dancing, but the dance that went to this song involved a girl/young woman with a ribbon dancing inside a ring till ties the ribbon around the arm of one of the boys/young men. He tries to flee but they end up dancing together in the middle of the ring. Although the lyric offered in this piano score starts *Och jungfrun hon gar i dansen* ('O maiden she goes dancing'), other versions refer to the circle in which the dancing is taking place: *Och jungfrun hon gar i ringen* ('O maiden she goes ring dancing'). *Hej, tomtegubbar* is another Swedish song associated with Christmas, but it was not dancing that was traditionally associated with this song but drinking. *Nu ha vi ljus här i vårt hus* is a song about Christmas eve, with lyrics by Rafael Hertzberg (1845-1896) and music by Johanna Ölander (1827-1909). Although a relatively recent composition it, like the first three of the above named dances, has come to have a ring dance associated with it and in the 1987 Ingmar Bergman movie *Fanny och Alexander* the family sing the song while dancing in a weaving line through the rooms of the house. The tune's also called *Julpolska* ('Christmas polska'—*polska* being the name for a much varied couples dance or triple time tune appropriate for that dance) which is appropriate for a tune that can serve well as a setting for two of my above couples dance.

The above medley was inspired by and cut out of a much longer medley arranged by Sune Waldimir under the title 'Julpotpurri' in a 1948 publication entitled on the cover *Nu är det Jul igen*, after the first song in the medley. I am indebted to pianist friend Sally Taylor for introducing me to this suite, for working with me on finding an arrangement that would work for a dance she invited me to devise, and for playing the chosen tunes so beautifully for our dancing pleasure at our Christmas Carol Ball in Canberra in 2019.

I have not matched traditions Swedish dance games or circles dances to the tunes we've used, as might be done at a party in Sweden, but have matched some mazurka-like couples dances of my own devising. Mazurka-like dances seemed appropriate as the Polish mazurka was possible being the ancestor of the Swedish *polska*. All three of the choreographies I describe are derived from dances I have published elsewhere. **Holiday Holubiec** in my *Dance Delights*, **Conjuring L'amour** and **Vulgarian Salutations** in my *Lost Dances of Earthly Delights*. I have adapted both the dances and the tune arrangements to be more complimentary of each other. From Waldimir's original suite we've omitted two of the original tunes, most of the originally intended tune repeats and some of the internal repeats, leaving us with 5 tunes each with 16 bars in 3/4 each. My 48-bar dance medley can be done once to the first three of the above tunes as arranged above, and danced a second time to the last two of the above five tunes, as arranged with the last tune (with no internal repeats) played twice. My intention is that dancers stay with the same partner for once through Dance 1, 2 and 3 and then at the end of 3 progress onto a new partner. If there are not enough confident dancers of the 48-bar sequence on the floor, you would be welcome to stay with your original partner and just repeat the whole sequence with them. If you don't want to engage in any on- night teaching and haven't prepared many dancers in advance, you could do a combination of my Dance 1 and 3 (skipping my slightly more challenging Dance 2), that two-dance 32 bar combination fitting 3 times within the medley as arranged above.

In my table above I have given the Swedish words (and a very rough translation) of one verse (and chorus if relevant) for each tune of the first four songs and two for the last song as it needs repeating to match the dance suite. I've not offered further verses above as the essential dance does not require them, but if you want to repeat the dance and have Swedish speakers sing different verses when a particular tune comes around again, you will find the extra verses in the piano score that I reproduce with permission from the original owned by Sally. My reproduction below is in a cut-down and somewhat squashed form with annotations to offer a playing guide that matches that I have offered in the transcription at the beginning of this entry.

Julpotpurri

Arr.: SUNE WALDIMIR

B- just x 1

band. Dem bin-der hon om sin kä-ras-tes arm. dem bin-der hon om sin kä-ras-tes arm. Och
hårt! Jag äm - nar ej att rym - ma bort, Jag äm - nar ej att rym - ma bort. Och
band. Så has-tigt den gos-sen åt sko-gen för svann, så has-tigt den gos-sen åt sko-gen för-svann. De
vär. Och vill du mig nå-got så har du mig här, och vill du mig nå-got så har du mig här. Och
man. Den vack-ras-te gos-sen i he-la vårt land, den vack-ras-te gos-sen i he-la vårt land.

A   E7   A   E7   A   F#   Hm   A   E7   A

AA- just x 1

5. Hej, tomtegubbar

land.   Hej, tom-te-gub-bar, slån i gla-sen och låt oss lus-ti-ga va - ra.   Hej, tom-te-gub-bar,

A   D   A7   D   A   D

BA- just x 1

slån i gla - sen och låt oss lus-ti-ga va - ra. En li-ten tid vi le-va här, med myc-ken mö-da och

D   A7   D   D   A   D   A   D

No repeat

stort be-svär.   Hej, tom-te-gub-bar slån i gla-sen och låt oss lus-ti-ga va - ra.

A   E7 A7   D   A7   D

Don't play the next song in score but play this next one twice through
with no internal repeats

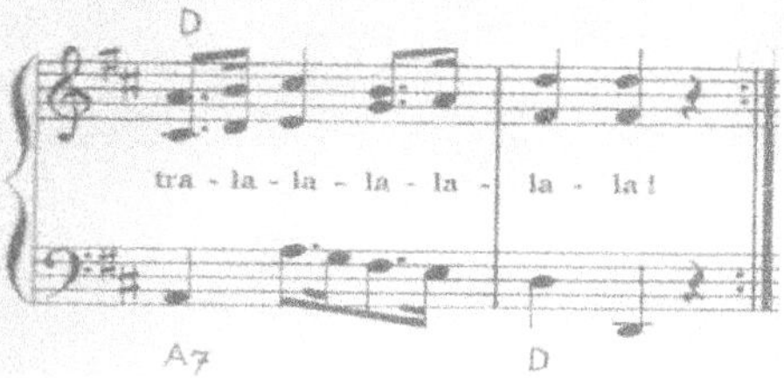

Nu ha vi ljus, här i vårt hus

1. Nu ha vi ljus här i vårt hus,
2. Kom, lil-la vän, kom nu i - gen!
3. Kom, ta en sväng! Klap-par i mängd

ju - len är kom-men, hopp, tra-la-la-la! Bar-nen i ring dan-sa om-kring, dan-sa om - kring.
Dan-sa kring gra-nen, hopp, tra-la-la-la! Gläd-jen är stor. Sys-ter och bror, sys-ter och bror,
jul-boc-ken häm-tat, hopp, tra-la-la-la! Lut-fisk och gröt, tär-ta så söt, tär-ta så söt,

No internal repeats

A7   D   A   Hm   E7   A

crescendo

Gra-nen står så grön och grann i stu-gan, gra-nen står så grön och grann i stu-gan. Tra-la-la-la-la, tra-la-la-la-la,
pap-pa, mamma, al-la gå i dan-sen, pap-pa, mamma, al-la gå i dan-sen.
få vi se-dan när vi slu-tat dan-sa, få vi se-dan när vi slu-tat dan-sa.

D   A7   D

tra-la-la-la-la-la-la-la!

Don't play the next two song in score but return to the top and play
all the above again

A7   D

John Gardiner-Garden, *The Christmas Carol Dance Book*, 2020

John Gardiner-Garden, *The Christmas Carol Dance Book*, 2020

www.ingramcontent.com/pod-product-compliance
Lightning Source LLC
Chambersburg PA
CBHW080843270326
41928CB00014B/2885